W9-BVS-022

HOT WORDS FOR THE SAT*

6th Edition

Linda Carnevale, M.A.

BARRON'S

*SAT is a registered trademark of the College Board, which was not involved in the production of, and does not endorse, this book.

Dedicated to

my beloved Sandro
& precious sons Phillip, Andrew, & Luca
who inspire me daily

~

my supportive family, friends, colleagues at
Cold Spring Harbor Schools, my wonderful students
~ and ~
my cherished parents
Anne & Ernest

ACKNOWLEDGMENTS

With love and gratitude to my husband and children, my inspirations. To my husband, who encouraged me every step of the way in this process, through late nights of writing, and who helped me find my way through myriad PC file management debacles.

With love to my parents, Anne and Ernest, who—since I was a preschooler—encouraged me to write, and to "dream the impossible dream."

Great thanks to my dedicated editor, Linda Turner, to Wayne Barr, who first welcomed me to Barron's, and to George Ehrenhaft for his contribution to this book.

Cartoon credit, page vii: "Zits" used with permission of the Zits Partnership, King Features Syndicate and the Cartoonist Group. All rights reserved.

All inquiries should be addressed to:
Barron's Educational Series, Inc.
250 Wireless Boulevard
Hauppauge, New York 11788
www.barronseduc.com

ISBN: 978-1-4380-0748-9

ISSN: 2327-1159

Printed in Canada
10 9 8 7 6 5 4 3 2 1

10%
POST-CONSUMER WASTE
Paper contains a minimum of 10% post-consumer waste (PCW). Paper used in this book was derived from certified, sustainable forestlands.

Contents

Introduction

Are you ready for the HOTTEST of the HOT WORDS?

This book is divided into 39 lessons, 37 containing more than 365 SAT-level words that have been taken off of Barron's high-frequency database of words and off of recent SAT tests. Additional SAT words are featured in the exercises.

The role of vocabulary on the new SAT

On the new SAT, effective March 2016, vocabulary remains pronounced. A strong, vast, and diverse vocabulary remains strongly beneficial to the test-taker. The vocabulary is both rich and varied, as the new SAT seeks to test a student's readiness for both college and career.

Beyond the SAT test, students will be tremendously edified by building a strong and broad vocabulary. This knowledge will enhance their enjoyment of success not only in college and career but also in life as they interact with their colleagues, contemporaries, and community members. Test or no test, an expansive and robust vocabulary is indispensible to all, regardless of one's choice of profession or life path.

Sentence completions have been eliminated

Although multiple-choice sentence completion questions will no longer appear on the SAT, as they used to in the old-format critical reading sections, they remain in this book as vocabulary-strengthening exercises. Work through these exercises diligently, as vocabulary improvement remains a relevant and significant component in scoring higher on the Reading, Writing and Language, and Essay sections of the SAT. Make flash cards for the words that are unfamiliar to you.

Why is this edition *particularly* HOT?

This edition contains a phonetic pronunciation guide for every word. Vocabulary-in-context paragraphs appear after each set of five lessons, illustrating how the SAT words can be used in descriptive prose. References have been updated and several definitions have been elaborated upon.

The innovative format of this book sets it apart from other vocabulary books. "**Word Clustering**" is especially effective in learning hundreds of vocabulary words. Unlike dictionary-style, alphabetized lists, clustering groups Hot Words with similar meanings so that distinctions in usage and connotation can become more apparent. *Never before presented so comprehensively in an SAT preparatory book, clustering boosts vocabulary building exponentially!*

In this edition: ACT vocabulary

There are four reading passages that make up the ACT Reading Test. The four passages come in four genres: Prose Fiction, Humanities, Social Science, and Natural Science. To clearly and thoroughly absorb the information in these expository passages, it is beneficial for test takers to have a strong vocabulary. Knowing more sophisticated words will allow test takers greater clarity about what they are reading and, in turn, allow them to answer questions more accurately. This edition of *Hot Words* includes two new ACT vocabulary lessons. The first lesson contains words appearing in the Prose Fiction and Humanities passages; the second lesson, the Social and Natural Sciences passages. In fact, these words all appear in *The Real ACT Prep Guide*, 3rd Edition, which is published by the ACT test makers themselves.

Vocabulary in your life

Vocabulary is still imperative and vital to doing well on the three critical reading sections of the SAT. Testing aside, gaining a broad and rich vocabulary edifies your life skills and people skills. The paragraphs that follow illustrate ways in which vocabulary can enrich your everyday life.

Future prep

If you apply to graduate school one day, the words you learn *now* will help you later on the verbal portions of grad school admissions exams, like the LSAT, MCAT, or GRE.

Reinforcement through writing

Next time you write an essay or creative piece for school, try to use some of your new words in your writing. If you have to submit a project on poster board or PowerPoint slides, include upper-level vocabulary words as you write out the text for this visual presentation. Use upper-level vocabulary in your e-mails and blogs.

Reinforcement through speaking

Be mindful when you participate in class or speak up at an after-school club or activity. Also be mindful when you speak to your parents, neighbors, or employer. Can you use new vocabulary words to get your points across more effectively as you engage in everyday conversations?

Lively letters

Next time you write a letter or thank-you note to Aunt Anne or Grandma Rose, include one or two of your new words in your message. Maybe you'll get a handwritten note back—more fun than getting a shorthand e-mail!

Zesty dinner talk

Sprinkle a couple of new words in your dinner conversation tonight. Did your teacher **lavish** you with high praise and an A+ ? Did the guest speaker at school refer to you as **astute**? Was your soccer team's spirit **bolstered** by a 9–1 win against the **formidable** Pythons? Go ahead and sprinkle those words . . . you might be offered a second helping of dessert!

What is exponential vocabulary growth?

Unlike linear growth, which involves a constant addend (+5 in this case)—5-10-15-20-25-30—exponential (or geometric) growth is rapid (×5 in this case)—5-25-125-625-3,125. As you can see, exponential sums far exceed linear sums. Linear vocabulary building involves learning one isolated, alphabetized word at a time. Exponential vocabulary building involves dynamically associated clusters of words. Consider this visual analogy: Linear vocabulary growth is like a tall stalk of bamboo, adding one foot of bamboo (or one word) at a time. Exponential vocabulary growth is like a massive oak tree, adding whole branches of words at a time.

The majority of lessons in this book are cluster-formatted so that you can expeditiously learn groups of words at the same time. As you work through each cluster lesson, read the definitions and illustrative sentences carefully. Challenge yourself to learn the nuance or shade of meaning for each individual word in the lesson.

Why cluster vocabulary words?

There are many reasons. Clustering is based on an educational-psychological idea called "apperception." Apperception, according to Merriam-Webster OnLine, is rooted in "the process of understanding something perceived in terms of previous experience" (knowledge). So, for example, if you know that *trite* and *banal* mean "unoriginal," link this "old" knowledge to "new" words like *platitude, hackneyed,* and *cliché.* Moreover, instead of regarding *platitude, hackneyed,* and *cliché* as isolated, unattached elements (as you'd encounter them in an A-B-C order list), think of this trio of words as linked to the same category that already contains *trite* and *banal.* Furthermore, apperception is "perception that reflects upon itself—sometimes intensified or energetic" (Merriam-Webster OnLine). Clustering in this manner keeps you immersed in SAT-type vocabulary, bringing your vocabulary growth to a new level.

Consider this analogy: Just as teachers of French or Spanish find immersion-style lessons effective, I find SAT-vocabulary immersion effective for me and for my students. Immerse yourself in SAT vocabulary. I hope that hearing a particular vocabulary word will bring to mind a bevy— a plethora—of associated words.

In each lesson of *Hot Words,* a connection exists among the words; the words relate to each other in some way. As a verbal SAT tutor, I have seen firsthand how this kind of vocabulary dynamic is highly effective for many of my students. When alphabetized lists are used, confusion and frustration sometimes occur for students because—as you can see—the words may start off in similar ways:

abberation	delectable	rebuff
abridge	delegate	rebuke
abrogate	deleterious	refute
abscond	delineate	rescind
abstain	deluge	revile
abstract	delusion	revoke

These look-alike/sound-alike words tend to get jumbled together, undermining our effort to learn hundreds of SAT-type words. Alphabetized lists are cumbersome, even trite. Unlike alphabetized lists, *cluster lists* are dynamic. Words that sound and look different can be closely related in meaning. An indispensable benefit of cluster learning is getting a close-up view of the subtleties of difference among the words featured in each lesson. Although challenging, this method is necessary for learning the real sense and usage of words.

Let's talk further about clustering and how this method of learning vocabulary relates to word recall. *Example:* I give you an *alphabetized list* of 25 words to memorize (five rock bands, five sports teams, five car brands, five fast foods, and five colleges). Then I ask you to memorize the list and recite back to me as many terms as you can remember.

Acura	Hot Dog	Pink
BMW	Jaguar	Pizza
Cheeseburger	Jets	Rangers
Columbia University	Knicks	Soft Pretzel
Fried Chicken	Loyola	Sting
Giants	Mets	The Cure
Guns n' Roses	New York University	University of
Harvard University	Nissan	Richmond
Honda	NSync	

How would you, personally, recall and recite these 25 terms?

Version A: Alphabetical

Acura	Hot Dog	Pink
BMW	Jaguar	Pizza
Cheeseburger	Jets	Rangers
Columbia University	Knicks	Soft Pretzel
Fried Chicken	Loyola	Sting
Giants	Mets	The Cure
Guns n' Roses	New York University	University of
Harvard University	Nissan	Richmond
Honda	NSync	

Version B: Random

Jets	Pink
Soft Pretzel	Hot Dog
Acura	Jaguar
Loyola	Harvard University
Guns n' Roses	Mets
Nissan	Giants
Fried Chicken	NSync
Sting	Cheeseburger
The Cure	New York University
Rangers	Knicks
Honda	University of Richmond
BMW	Columbia University
Pizza	

Version C: Clustered

Jets	Loyola	Jaguar
Knicks	University of Richmond	BMW
Giants	Columbia University	Honda
Mets	New York University	Nissan
Rangers	Harvard University	Acura

Pizza	The Cure
Soft Pretzel	Pink
Hot Dog	Sting
Fried Chicken	Guns n' Roses
Cheeseburger	NSync

For the most part, our brains work and think by associating things that are alike. Clusters and categories are natural to us in terms of how the majority of us learn. Think back to preschool. Did you learn about colors, shapes, and animals simultaneously? Or, did you learn colors, then shapes, then animals, then letters, and so on? Effective learning is not a staccato, haphazard, mumbo-jumbo process that just happens to occur in A-B-C order. Learning is ordered in a way that makes sense.

As you will see as you work through this book, cluster lessons are not made of pure synonyms. Yes, the words relate to a theme or general idea, but the lists compel you to learn the subtle differences in usage and their nuances of meaning. The three illustrative sentences provided with each word help you do just this. Based on my students' oral and written testimony to me, week after week, I am convinced that clustering is more effective than basic alphabetized lists.

Clusters are effective. If clustered or theme-based vocabulary is new to you, I suggest you try the bonus section that this book contains: Mini Vocabulary Clusters (see Appendix A). These bite-size groups of related words will familiarize you with the cluster concept and warm you up for the lessons that contain larger groups of theme-related words.

Memory Tips is a popular and exciting part of *Hot Words*. At the end of each lesson, I show you how to capitalize on your memory and how to harness the meanings of a plethora of SAT words. *Hot Words* shows you practical memory techniques (known as mnemonics) that you can apply to your vocabulary building. Memory Tips show you how resourcefulness and creativity—as well as knowledge of prefixes and root words—can help you amass a large, upper-level vocabulary.

Research shows that memory works predominantly by linking something new or unknown to some knowledge that you already have. Linking an SAT word (the unknown) to some word you already know is an effective method for the daunting task of learning hundreds of upper-level words. Many memory tips work this way—by linking the *new* to the *known*. Other tips, as you'll see, use additional approaches that are just as effective. Some examples are letter clusters, word roots, prefixes/suffixes, slant rhymes, word pictures, and chants.

As you work through each lesson, *read aloud* the words, definitions, and sample sentences so that your auditory learning mode is engaged. Be aware of making distinctions in meaning between words that have similar definitions. Try using the words in sentences that you make up on your own.

What role does vocabulary play in the SAT?

Vocabulary is more important than ever. The SAT asks students to compose a "writing sample," so students' vocabulary skills matter a great deal. The College Board asks students to write a persuasive-type essay—an effective and compelling expository essay requires a strong, rich vocabulary.

The critical reading passages are saturated with upper-level vocabulary, and the questions and answer choices also contain high-level vocabulary.

Sentence completions have answer choices brimming with upper-level vocabulary. Moreover, most questions feature challenging vocabulary within the sentences themselves. More often than not, these vocabulary words function as context clues for the blanks. Not knowing key words that appear within the sentences can hamper your ability to answer correctly.

A strong and vast vocabulary remains a primary requisite for a competitive verbal score.

Use a vocabulary notebook

Purchase a marble-bound or journal-type notebook that you devote to vocabulary building, or create a vocabulary document on your iPad. Pick a notebook whose cover and size appeal to you. Your vocabulary notebook will be a companion to *Hot Words for the SAT*. Every lesson contains memory tips that use a variety of strategies to help you remember words. Write the memory tips in your vocabulary notebook, underlining or highlighting word roots, prefixes, or letter clusters, as shown in the memory tips.

Once you get the hang of using memory clues, come up with memory clues of your own. In order to work efficiently, only invent memory clues for words that challenge you. It would be a waste of time to think up memory clues for words that you already know. As you work through each lesson, add the tips I give to your notebook, and spend some time inventing your own memory devices. After all, you have special knowledge that's unique to you: your cultural heritage, travel, a foreign language, a hobby, an instrument, and so on. Your "special knowledge" can help you come up with memory tips that no one else can.

Let your vocabulary notebook be colorful and lively! Underline or highlight parts of the words! Use color and highlighters! Draw pictures to help make associations. Clip out vocabulary words that you spot in newspapers and magazines and paste them into your notebook. I recommend you clip and paste the entire phrase or headline, for example, so that the word has a context. Read through the words and tips in your vocabulary notebook each day. This ritual will solidify the meanings of new words for you as you build a strong and vital vocabulary.

Create homemade flash cards

Certainly, you can purchase a box or two of flash cards at the bookstore. In fact, you will have a variety from which to choose. However, the original flash cards that you create for yourself are typically most effective. Your preexisting knowledge, your wit, your sense of humor, and your personal associations will come through on *your* flash cards, providing that you add an engaging mnemonic device (memory aid) to each card.

I recommend this format: Write the word neatly (*and correctly spelled*) on the front of the index card. On the back of the card, include the following:

- A concise definition (primary and secondary, whenever possible)
- One or two SAT-level synonyms (look for synonyms toward the end of the definition, or use a thesaurus)
- A mnemonic device (memory aid) that you have devised

To read examples of various types of mnemonics, review the memory tips provided at the end of each lesson in *Hot Words for the SAT*. Be a kid again, and use color: markers, highlighters, colored pencils, colored ink!

Picasso or not, you can enhance your flash cards with a sketch or doodle that illustrates some aspect of your memory aid. This added, aesthetic touch draws upon your visual sense, which, for many, is their strongest learning modality.

Pronunciation guide

This sixth edition of *Hot Words for the SAT* includes a user-friendly, phonetic pronunciation guide for each word. The pronunciations provided do not require you to know how to read enigmatic diacritical markings, which often include symbolic notations such as acute accents, grave accents, macrons, circumflex, and tilde. For many students, these markings are unfamiliar and, frankly, not that helpful. The pronunciations provided in this new edition are based on the first pronunciation (if there is more than one for a particular meaning) recommended and preferred by our reference standard, *Merriam-Webster's Collegiate Dictionary, Eleventh Edition*.

Read aloud the pronunciation note, just as it sounds. If you are unsure about how a word is pronounced, ask someone—a parent, a grandparent, a teacher, an older sibling—to say the word aloud to you for clarification. Hyphens indicate syllable breaks. Stress or accentuate the syllable that is fully capitalized. You will "hear" the word pronounced correctly. This pronunciation guide is valuable because using these words in your everyday speech—and pronouncing them correctly—is one goal of this book. If you are unsure about the accuracy of your oral recitations of the words, try vocalizing the words aloud to a teacher, another adult, an older sibling, or a study partner. More often than not, two pairs of ears are better than one.

Vocabulary-in-context paragraphs

For every set of five lessons, this edition now features lively para-graphs within the review exercises that contain words appearing in the prior five lessons. For added edification, additional words from other lessons may appear boldfaced within these narratives. In those cases, the lesson numbers are indicated in parentheses. In light of a particular paragraph's theme and context, the meanings of the bold-faced words should be clear. If you find, however, that you are uncer-tain about the meanings, review the words' definitions and illustrative sentences, as provided within the referenced lessons in *Hot Words for the SAT*.

Sentence completion exercises

Each set of five lessons includes a sentence completion exercise that features both single and double blanks. Please note that part of your task is to select the best word for the blank, based not only on the word's meaning but also on the word's part of speech (noun, adjec-tive, adverb, verb). If you are unsure about a particular word's part of speech, return to the lesson in which the part of speech is indicated (*n., adj., adv., vb.*) right after the word's pronunciation guide. As the sentence completion directions state: *Select a word form and part of speech that fit correctly within the sentence.*

F ind context clues and key words within the sentences.

Context clues are words or phrases within the sentence that indicate what meaning the blank requires. For example, "unwilling to compro-mise" could indicate *willful*, "big-hearted and generous" could indicate *magnanimous,* and "without a word" could indicate *taciturn.* Key words include opposite-indicators like *although, despite*, and *even though*. Key words also include negatives such as *not*, *hardly*, and *without.*

E stimate the meaning of the word for the blank(s).

Before fishing around the five answer choices, make it a habit to guess or predict the meaning of the blank. This way, you will be less misguided by false positives, decoys, and traps in the answer choices. Think first; then look.

W rite a positive (+) or negative (−) sign on the blank to indicate the word's value.

Word values are based on your "feel" for the word. A word's subtle undertone of meaning and its connotation make up its word value. If you get the sense that the meaning required by the blank has a negative or uncomplimentary meaning or connotation, simply cross off all the positive-type words. Word values allow you to effectively use the process of elimination and narrow in on the correct answer.

These **FEW** steps can help you become proficient at correctly answering sentence completion questions.

Note: *The answer choices for these sentence completions come from vocabulary that appears within the lesson. Answer choices can be the lesson words themselves, or words that appear in definitions or memory tips. Read the sentences carefully, getting a sense of how they flow. Then, be sure to select an answer whose word form or part of speech fits correctly within the context of the sentence.*

Wishing you the best,
Linda Carnevale, M.A.
Alumna, Columbia University's Teachers College

Lesson 1

CAT GOT YOUR TONGUE?
Words Relating to Using Few Words or Being Quiet

brevity concise laconic pithy quiescent reticent
succinct taciturn terse

brevity (BREV-ih-tee) *n.* briefness or conciseness in speech or writing

For the sake of **brevity**, choose your words with care.

Limited space in the newsletter makes **brevity** essential.

When time is short, **brevity** is a virtue.

concise (cun-SISE) *adj.* using few words in speaking or writing

A **concise** explanation is preferable to a long-winded one.

Leslie's essay is pretty wordy; she should try to be more **concise**.

For a **concise** summary of the book, read the book jacket.

laconic (luh-CAHN-ik) *adj.* using few words in speech

Because the senator's **laconic** reply lacked specificity, it raised more questions than it answered.

It was just too hot to give more than a **laconic** response to the question.

Ms. Allen's **laconic** explanation consisted of a single word: pepperoni.

pithy (PIH-thee) *adj.* brief and full of meaning and substance; concise

For the yearbook, Jenny searched online for **pithy** quotations about courage.

Jonathan's sonnet ended with a **pithy** rhyming couplet.

What expresses affection more **pithily** than the three words, *I love you*?

1

quiescent (kwy-EH-sunt) *adj.* quiet; still; inactive

Mount St. Helens has been **quiescent** since its last eruption in 1986.

On long summer weekends, the city loses its bustle and is strangely **quiescent**.

Never one to make waves, Leo **quiescently** followed the coach's orders.

reticent (RET-ih-sunt) *adj.* not talking much; reserved

Usually **reticent**, Ms. Worthy surprised us all with a long story at lunch.

Tom and Molly are a mismatched pair; he's shy and **reticent**, but she never stops talking.

I thought the old man was **reticent**, but he wouldn't talk because he had no teeth.

succinct (suk-SINKT) *adj.* clearly and briefly stated; concise

Mr. Phillips asked us to write a **succinct** summary of our term papers.

The title **succinctly** conveys the point of my paper.

Let me state this as **succinctly** as I can: "No late papers."

taciturn (TAS-ih-turn) *adj.* silent; sparing of words; close-mouthed

Next to me on the bus sat a **taciturn** girl who said nothing during the four-hour ride.

Throughout the party, Larry was moody and **taciturn**. No one heard a peep from him.

Mom kept quiet, not because she's **taciturn**, but because she refused to make the decision for me.

terse (TURS) *adj.* using only the words that are needed to make the point; very concise, sometimes to the point of rudeness

Mia wanted details about Joyce's new boyfriend, but got only a **terse** description.

Terse speakers make dull lecturers.

The principal's **terse** reply was clear: "No dogs at school."

Personality (Humans)

MEMORY TIPS Fennwords Characteristic Rudeness
(Stuff)

Use these mnemonics (memory devices) to boost your vocabulary. Make up your own memory clues for words in this lesson that are challenging for you. Add these tips—and your own—to your Vocabulary Notebook.

brevity Connect this word to a related word that you most likely already know: **abbreviate**. Notice how both words share the letter cluster *brev*!

pithy Think of just the *pit* (central part) of the topic and nothing more. Remember that **pithy** expressions are substantial and to the point.

quiescent Did you notice that the word *quiet* is within **quiescent**? Use this to see the definition within the word: still; inactive; quiet. In your Vocabulary Notebook, underline or highlight q-u-i-e-t in **quiescent**. Another SAT-level word, ac**quiesce**, is related to **quiescent**. Acquiesce means "to peaceably agree or quietly give in to."

taciturn In Latin *tacitus* means silent. *Tacit* means implied or expressed without words, as in a "tacit agreement."

MATCHING

Match the vocabulary words in Column A with *one or more* of their defining characteristics appearing in Column B.

Column A

1. quiescent

2. pithy

3. concise

4. terse

5. taciturn

Column B

a. inactive or still

b. to the point

c. using few words to express oneself

d. quiet and reserved

e. brief, almost to the point of rudeness

SENTENCE COMPLETION

Remember: Answer choices can be the lesson words themselves, or words that appear in definitions or Memory Tips. Select a word form and part of speech that fit correctly within the sentence.

1. Gabe is a master of _____ because he can usually get his point across in three words or less!
(tersely, reticence, abbreviation, pithiness, laconic)

2. _____ people make me feel uncomfortable; they are so quiet and disengaged that it makes them hard to read.
(Succinct, Reservedly, Reticent, Concise, Brevity)

3. After being asked repeatedly to go on a movie date, Julian _____ responded, "Not interested," to the girl on the other end of the phone.
(quiescently, reservedly, concise, brevity, tersely)

4. Known for her _____, Hailey delivered a 40-second speech that pithily emphasized the many reasons why she would be the best pick for student government president.
(reticence, brevity, terseness, taciturn, abbreviations)

5. Far from a blabbermouth, Tina is as _____ a young lady as one can find.
(succinct, pithy, taciturn, concisely, acquiescent)

WORDS IN CONTEXT

Based on the context in which each **bold** word is used, identify the word usage of each sentence as either C (Correct) or I (Incorrect).

1. The mayor was commended for his **pithy** speech. He made meaningful points during a mere half-hour delivery.

2. The gabby shop owner welcomed **laconic** exchanges with customers.

3. Since space was limited, the advertising executive instructed copywriters to write **concise** photo captions.

4. Unlike their customary drawn-out explanations, the Grants related the story of the burglary **tersely**.

5. **Succinct** gossip is the most painful; it hurts its subjects more than any other type of rumor.

bombastic circumlocution colloquial diffuse digress
eloquence garrulous grandiloquent loquacious prattle
ramble rant rhetorical verbose voluble

bombastic (bom-BAS-tic) *adj.* using language in a pompous, showy way; speaking to impress others

Luke's speech was so **bombastic**; was he speaking to communicate or simply to show off?

Putting on airs, the **bombastic** orator used a bunch of big words that basically said nothing at all.

"Keep your language simple and honest," urged the English teacher. "**Bombast** in writing or speaking is ostentatious. In other words, high-flown language is unacceptable."

circumlocution (sir-kum-low-Q-shun) *n.* speaking in circles; round-about speech

To avoid hurting anyone's feelings, Hank resorted to **circumlocution**.

Circumlocution is commonly called *beating around the bush*.

The principal said, "Your **circumlocution** is wasting time. Just tell me exactly what you saw out in the parking lot."

colloquial (kuh-LOW-kwee-ul) *adj.* pertaining to common everyday speech; conversational

The book is filled with **colloquial** expressions that reflect the speech of people in the deep South.

Two examples of **colloquial** greetings are "Hey, dude, how's it goin'?" and "What's up, man?"

Sometimes a **colloquial** word becomes standard in English usage.

diffuse (dih-FEWS) *adj.* spread out, not concise; wordy

The class discussion was so **diffuse** that few solid points were made.

"This essay lacks focus," said the teacher. "It's too **diffuse**."

A **diffuse** argument won't convince the class to vote for me.

digress (die-GRES) *vb.* to wander off from the subject or topic spoken about

We don't have time to **digress** from the main issue right now.

The **digressions** in Carl's speech interested me more than the main topic.

Mr. Helms habitually **digresses** from the point of the lesson.

eloquence (EH-low-kwens) *n.* artful ease with speaking; speech that can influence people's feelings

Even the most **eloquent** graduation speeches are quickly forgotten.

Although he sounds **eloquent**, he is still full of hot air.

Among American presidents, Lincoln wins the prize for **eloquence**.

garrulous (GAR-u-lus) *adj.* talkative; loquacious

Garrulous gatherings of students are unwelcome in a library that values silence.

Garrulous merrymakers gather in Times Square on New Year's Eve.

Our sightseeing guide was so **garrulous** that we never got to enjoy the serenity of the mountain lake.

grandiloquent (gran-DIH-luh-kwent) *adj.* using big and fancy words when speaking for the purpose of impressing others

"Instead of **grandiloquence**," cautioned the teacher, "use plain language."

Mr. Green tries to impress students with his **grandiloquence** instead of telling them what they need to know.

Mickey used **grandiloquent** language to conceal his ignorance of the subject.

loquacious (low-KWAY-shus) *adj.* very talkative; liking to talk; garrulous

The **loquacious** audience grew quiet when the movie started.

Have you ever met a lawyer who wasn't **loquacious**?

Loquacity was not Steve's strength; he was quiet and subdued.

prattle (PRA-tl) *vb.* to speak on and on in a senseless and silly manner; to talk foolishly

The **prattle** of freshmen resounded through the cafeteria.

"Stop **prattling**," urged Ms. Ham. "I can't understand a word you're saying."

After twenty straight hours in the car, their intelligent conversation turned into **prattle**.

ramble (RAM-bul) *vb.* to talk on and on pointlessly, without clear direction

Rambling on and on, Harold lost his audience's attention; his listeners had no idea what he was talking about.

The teacher **rambled** endlessly about various unrelated topics.

A wandering, unfocused mind is one trait of a **rambler**.

rant (RANT) *vb.* to talk very loudly, even wildly; rave

Because the speaker **ranted** on and on, the audience stopped listening after a while.

Upset by plummeting sales, the boss stormed into the office and **ranted** at her sales staff, "We're on the verge of bankruptcy!"

Ranting is far from a polite way to get your point across.

rhetorical (re-TOR-uh-kul) *adj.* relating to speech that is used to persuade or have some effect; insincere in expression

The speech of politicians is often thick with **rhetoric**.

The attorney's forceful **rhetoric** convinced the jury to acquit the defendant.

Metaphors, allusions, and pithy quotations are examples of **rhetorical** devices.

verbose (vur-BOSE) *adj.* using too many words; wordy; long-winded

> The teacher asked Brenda to cut her **verbose** speech from 40 to 15 minutes.

> When time is short, **verbose** explanations are inappropriate.

> Some English teachers call **verbose** writing "flabby."

voluble (VOL-you-bul) *adj.* talking a great deal with ease; glib

> Victor is such a **voluble** speaker that it takes him a half hour to answer a simple question.

> Sean always has been shy around girls, but he's trying to be more **voluble**.

> Unlike her more **voluble** opponent, Ollie gave short and well-focused speeches during the election campaign.

MEMORY TIPS

Use these mnemonics (memory devices) to boost your vocabulary. Make up your own memory clues for words in this lesson that are personally challenging. Add these tips—and your own—to your Vocabulary Notebook.

loc-, loq- These word roots relate to speaking. Notice how they appear in five words in this lesson: **circumlocution, colloquial, eloquence, grandiloquent,** and **loquacious.**

garrulous Think of "**garrulous** gorillas" in the jungle and how noisy and *talkative* they are! Use "**Garrulous** gorillas! **Garrulous** gorillas! **Garrulous** gorillas!" as an alliterative chant; say it aloud three times in a row! Write this chant three times in your Vocabulary Notebook.

prattle In your mind's eye, picture a baby playing with *rattles* while she **prattles.** Once again, take advantage of the letter clusters (and sometimes words) that naturally occur within the vocabulary words. This visual mnemonic is highly memorable since it creates a fun-loving, even silly, picture in your mind's eye.

voluble Be careful with this word. Do *not* think about volume in terms of loudness of speech; instead, think about volume in terms of *quantity* or *amount* of speech. In other words, Victor can be speaking **volubly** while he is whispering. **Voluble** means glib—not loud. Get it?

MATCHING

Match the vocabulary words in Column A with *one or more* of their defining characteristics appearing in Column B.

Column A

1. garrulous
2. prattle
3. eloquence
4. rant
5. voluble

Column B

a. to speak loudly, almost yelling
b. using many words
c. emotionally stirring speech
d. silly talk
e. very talkative

SENTENCE COMPLETION

Remember: Answer choices can be the lesson words themselves, or words that appear in definitions or Memory Tips. Select a word form and part of speech that fit correctly within the sentence.

1. _____ on and on at record speed about nonsense, Desiree left her listeners with no clue as to what she was talking about, but left them transfixed by her bright red motoring lips.
   (Prattling, Diffusing, Volubly, Ranting, Eloquently)

2. Poised and _____, Lucille was born for the actor's playhouse and podium.
   (digressive, rhetorical, colloquial, bombastic, loquacious)

3. Tonight's dinner conversation was downright _____; I was unable to recall even a morsel of wisdom or substance.
   (colloquial, grandiloquent, diffuse, ramble, garrulous)

4. _____ is a communications skill that can get one places, especially if he or she wants to go into news broadcasting or radio announcing.
   (Prattle, Eloquence, Verbosity, Circumlocution, Ranting)

5. Juan observed that speakers who tend to _____ from their topics have more light-hearted and carefree personalities, while those
   who unconditionally stay on course tend to be more uptight and serious.
   (digress, circumlocutory, rant, glib, bombast)

WORDS IN CONTEXT

Based on the context in which each **bold** word is used, identify the word
usage of each sentence as either C (Correct) or I (Incorrect).

1. Deep thought is behind **prattling**.

2. Contrary to popular belief, **ranting** is very peaceful.

3. "**Verbose** speech will be penalized for its long and drawn-out character," said the debate coach.

4. Political candidates can benefit from an **eloquent** manner of
   speaking.

5. **Garrulous** partygoers huddled in the den corner, observing the crowd
   quietly.

Lesson 3

THE HIGH AND MIGHTY
Words Relating to Feeling Superior

arrogant braggart complacent contemptuous disdainful egotistical elitist haughty insolent narcissistic ostentatious presumptuous pretentious supercilious swagger

---

arrogant (ER-uh-gunt) *adj.* overbearing; proud; haughty

- Peter's **arrogance** annoyed his classmates, who thought he was vain and conceited.

  His **arrogant** attitude made it hard for others to warm up to him.

  The dog looked like its master, **arrogant** and proud—not the sort of pet to cuddle with.

braggart (BRA-gurt) *n.* one who boasts a great deal; one likely to self-aggrandize

- Leo cannot help being a **braggart**. He boasts all day about his exploits on the basketball court.

  Even if you are a champion swimmer, avoid sounding like a **braggart** on your college application essay.

  Although Tanya is very proud of her talents, she isn't a **braggart**.

complacent (kum-PLAY-snt) *adj.* self-satisfied; smug

- **Complacent** in his role as an assistant dean, Mr. Rogers did not aspire to become a principal.

  Carole could get an A in math, but she's too **complacent** to work for it.

  Complacence destroys ambition.

contemptuous (kun-TEMP-choo-us) *adj.* lacking respect; scornful

- Accustomed to filet mignon, Fido glared **contemptuously** at the bowl of dog chow in front of him.

11

When rival cliques are **contemptuous** of each other, there's going to be trouble.

Parents should teach tolerance, not breed **contempt** for people's differences.

disdainful (dis-DANE-ful) *adj.* full of bitter scorn and pride; aloof

The audience showed its **disdain** by heckling the singer who couldn't carry a tune.

When asked for a dollar for a cup of coffee, Mrs. Snodbrow eyed the panhandler **disdainfully**.

I can't keep my **disdainful** comments to myself when Emily deliberately acts foolishly to get attention.

egotistical (ee-guh-TIS-tih-kul) *adj.* excessively self-absorbed; very conceited

Egotistical individuals cannot get enough of their own reflections in the mirror.

Nathan is so **egotistical**; he thinks every girl on campus wants to meet him.

The **egotistical** student could not understand why he was not voted most popular by the senior class.

elitist (ay-LEE-tist) *adj.* snobbish, condescending; highbrow in the manner in which one speaks or carries oneself

"**Elitist** comments are neither acceptable nor welcome in this home," announced Ms. Kindred, who valued both kindness and equity.

An **elitist** attitude can ostracize friends, leading to a life of loneliness and strife.

Kian boasted endlessly about his academic qualifications, demonstrating his **elitist** mindset.

haughty (HAW-tee) *adj.* having great pride in oneself and dislike for others

Ralph struts around like a proud rooster. His **haughtiness** keeps him from making friends.

Haughty Hannah has no use for others; she's too busy thinking and talking about herself.

The folks next door are too **haughty** for a Ford; they drive only Mercedes and BMWs.

insolent (IN-suh-lunt) *adj.* boldly disrespectful in speech or behavior; rude

- When Ernie told the principal to "bug off," his **insolence** earned him a suspension from school.

"No **insolent** remarks on the ball field," warned the coach. "Teammates must respect each other, even when they strike out."

Before she met that wild crowd, Megan was quiet and demure; now she's an **insolent**, foul-mouthed roughneck.

narcissistic (nar-suh-SIS-tik) *adj.* having to do with extreme self-adoration and a feeling of superiority to everyone

- Becky is so **narcissistic**, she even chooses her friends based on how their looks complement hers.

Quentin is a full-fledged **narcissist**; he spends half the day in front of a mirror adoring himself.

Feeling good about yourself is healthy, but when self-esteem turns to **narcissism**, you've got a problem.

ostentatious (ahs-tun-TAY-shus) *adj.* having to do with showing off; pretentious

- Don't you agree that wearing a pearl bracelet, two ruby rings, and diamond-studded earrings is a bit **ostentatious**?

Meredith talks about nothing but her father's yacht, ski trips to Aspen, Club Med vacations, and other **ostentatious** displays of wealth.

My parents prefer staying at a quiet inn by the sea to a glitzy, **ostentatious** Miami Beach hotel.

presumptuous (prih-ZUM-choo-us) *adj.* too forward or bold; overstepping proper bounds

Isn't it **presumptuous** of Julie to expect all her friends to do only what *she* wants to do on Friday nights?

Presumptuous people would be better off with a bit of self-control and tact.

- On his first day of work, Harris **presumptuously** asked his boss, "When do I get a raise?"

pretentious (pri-TEN-shus) *adj.* claiming or pretending increased importance; ostentatious; affectedly grand

My neighbors thrive on **pretension**. They plaster their windshields with the decals of posh prep schools, beach clubs, and Ivy League colleges.

- **Pretentious** Patrick never goes anywhere without a copy of *Ulysses* under his arm, even though he's never read a word of it.

Isn't **pretension** often a mask for self-doubt?

supercilious (soo-pur-SIH-lee-us) *adj.* looking down on others; proud and scornful

While strutting to class with her nose in the air, **supercilious** Sue notices no one.

If we held a contest for **superciliousness**, haughty Hannah would win hands down.

- "Success depends on everyone working together as equals," explained Esther. "No one with a **supercilious** attitude is welcome."

swagger (SWA-gur) *vb.* to walk around in a proud, showy manner; to boast in a loud manner

Butch's **swagger** reveals an ego as big as a house.

Walking around the school with his customary **swagger**, Pat conveys the impression that he owns the place.

- Mike and Gus acted like guests of honor at the party, **swaggering** from room to room.

MEMORY TIPS

Use these mnemonics (memory devices) to boost your vocabulary. Make up your own memory clues for words in this unit that are personally challenging. Add these tips—and your own—to your Vocabulary Notebook. Remember, vocabulary building is key to increasing your score on the verbal SAT.

haughty This chant is catchy and helpful: "It's naughty to be **haughty**! It's naughty to be **haughty**! It's naughty to be **haughty**!" Repeated three times in succession, the chant emphasizes the negative connotation of this word. Haughtiness is an undesirable character trait.

narcissistic Have you heard about the good-looking Greek guy named Narcissus? Narcissus falls in love with his own reflection! He stays lakeside forever, gazing adoringly, until he withers and dies. If that isn't self-loving and self-adoring, what is?

pretentious Let the first six letters of this word lead you to its meaning. Think of it this way: **Pretentious** is about pretending to be more than you are. See, it's as if the meaning is built into the word!

supercilious Connect this word to superior. People who behave in a **supercilious** or superior manner feel they are above (*super* means above) others.

MATCHING

Match the vocabulary words in Column A with *one or more* of their defining characteristics in Column B. Remember, some words may have more than one correct answer.

Column A	Column B
1. disdainful	a. overly proud; disliking others
2. complacent	b. smug
3. haughty	c. a boastful individual
4. pretentious	d. disrespectful
5. braggart	e. pretending to be more important than you are

SENTENCE COMPLETION

Remember: Answer choices can be the lesson words themselves, or words that appear in definitions or Memory Tips. Select a word form and part of speech that fit correctly within the sentence.

1. Peter has a (an) _____ air about him; when he speaks to his colleagues, it's as if he addresses them from up on a big, high horse.
   (swaggering, braggart, insolent, narcissism, disdainful)

2. "Bold and _____ conduct won't get you farther than the detention room or the demerit list," Mr. McKee admonished as he looked sharply into the bully's eyes.
   (egotistical, smug, haughty, complacent, insolent)

3. Ms. Bula would no longer put up with her supervisor's _____ attitude toward her, for she would not let herself get knocked down another peg!
(presumptuous, haughtiness, aloof, swaggering, supercilious)

4. Ever since Mitchell made the runway at Bryant Park, he struts around with a broad-shouldered _____ that says, "Check me out; I'm all that!"
(ostentatious, egotistical, swagger, complacency, braggart)

5. _____ Hunter has no friends; every time he talks, he mentions his latest athletic accolades, academic accomplishments, or financial windfalls.
(Scornful, Presumptuous, Egotistically, Insolent, Pretentious)

WORDS IN CONTEXT

Based on the context in which each **bold** word is used, identify the word usage of each sentence as either C (Correct) or I (Incorrect).

1. Above all, Mia's **supercilious** attitude shows her generosity of spirit.

2. **Arrogance** results from an individual's selflessness.

3. Rudeness is one component of **insolence**.

4. For the braggart, showiness and **pretension** go hand in hand.

5. A **complacent** youth has a great desire to learn from the experience of others.

<table>
<tr><td>**Lesson 4**</td><td># THAT'S ALL BEEN SAID BEFORE! BORING . . . ZZZZ
Words Relating to Unoriginal, Dull, Played Out</td></tr>
</table>

banal cliché derivative hackneyed insipid lackluster
mundane pedestrian platitude prosaic trite vapid

---

banal (buh-NAL) *adj.* dull or stale because of overuse; trite; hackneyed

To wake up and realize your adventure was all a dream is a **banal** ending for a short story.

Have you heard the **banal** joke about the moron who threw the clock out the window in order to see time fly?

Banality is boring because it's so predictable.

cliché (klee-SHAY) *n.* an idea or expression that has become stale due to overuse

"I'm so hungry I could eat a *rhinoceros*," gives an original twist to an old **cliché**.

Good writers avoid **clichés** like the plague.

Lazy writers rely on **clichés** because it's hard work to express ideas with fresh, new phrases.

derivative (diy-RIH-vuh-tiv) *adj.* unoriginal; taken from something already existing

"Write an original sci-fi story," instructed Mr. Schirmer, "not **derivative** fiction drawn from *2001: A Space Odyssey* or *The Time Machine*."

Instead of presenting her unique artistic vision, Julie's **derivative** work resembled the paintings of the old masters.

English is a **derivative** language. It is made up of words that originated in many other languages.

hackneyed (HAK-need) *adj.* made commonplace by overuse; trite (*n.* hack, one who copies or imitates the work of others)

Miss Cole, our poetry teacher, said, "Because poets aim to create new insights, they shun **hackneyed** language."

- Then she added, "If you think imaginatively, you'll avoid **hackneyed** phrases such as *ruby lips* and *rosy-fingered dawn*."

Only **hack** writers rely on **hackneyed** expressions. That's what makes them **hacks**.

insipid (in-SIH-pud) *adj.* lacking flavor or taste; unexciting

- The conversation at dinner was so **insipid** that Monica fell asleep at the table.

What kept the Hagans from going to church on Sunday morning was the minister, whose **insipid** sermons made them want to go back to bed.

- What I thought would be a scary movie turned out to be an **insipid** story of a harmless ghost.

lackluster (LAK-luhs-ter) *adj.* lacking vitality, energy, or brightness; boring

Laura's **lackluster** grades may prevent her from going to a top college.

Lackluster teachers who cannot engage their students' interest give this school a bad name.

- Even a superior actor finds it challenging to enliven a **lackluster** script.

mundane (muhn-DAYN) *adj.* commonplace; ordinary

In contrast to the new and unusual, the **mundane** happenings of everyday existence are pretty dull.

- Woolf is an author who can find something magical even in such a **mundane** activity as brushing one's teeth.

The movies offer an escape from the **mundane** character of daily life.

pedestrian (peh-DES-tree-un) *adj.* commonplace, ordinary, unoriginal, mundane

- **Pedestrian** thinkers contributed lackluster ideas to the Socratic seminar.

Her **pedestrian** screenplay did not grab an iota of attention from the sitcom's co-producers.

Make your college application essay attention grabbing and compelling; nothing admissions officers dislike more than having to read another sleepy sample of **pedestrian** prose.

platitude (PLA-tuh-tood) *n.* quality of being dull; an obvious remark uttered as if it were original

- How Rick's poem won an award for originality boggles my mind, since it consists of nothing but **platitudes**.

A **platitude** is as enriching intellectually as last month's bread is satisfying nutritionally.

A recipe to induce sleep is a monotonous voice and a plethora of **platitudes**.

prosaic (pro-ZAY-ik) *adj.* dull; commonplace

The novel *Mr. and Mrs. Bridge* is an indictment of an ordinary American couple who lead the dullest, most **prosaic** life imaginable.

- A **prosaic** Sunday morning means sleeping late and lingering over a big pancake breakfast while browsing the Sunday newspaper.

What is more **prosaic** than a movie and pizza on a Friday night?

trite (TRITE) *adj.* unoriginal and stale due to overuse

Because my essay was filled with clichés, Mr. Gill red-penciled "**trite**" all over it.

- When Bob asked what I thought of getting up at 4 A.M., only the **tritest** response came to me: "Well, they say the early bird catches the worm."

Mr. Gill claims that **triteness** is a sign of an air-filled brain.

vapid (VA-pid) *adj.* lacking freshness and zest; flat; stale

Behind every uninspiring, **vapid** TV sitcom, you'll find an empty-headed producer, director, and screenwriter.

Tired of **vapid** advertising gimmicks, the company resorted to sky-writing to promote its newest line of swimwear.

The speaker's **vapid** delivery emptied the conference hall within 10 minutes.

MEMORY TIPS

Use these mnemonics (memory devices) to boost your vocabulary. Make up your own memory clues for words in this lesson that are personally challenging. Add these tips—and your own—to your Vocabulary Notebook. Remember, vocabulary building is key to increasing your score on the verbal SAT.

banal You can spell *bla* from **banal**, right? Now, let *bla* be the connection to boring; *boring* is a solid definition for **banal**.

lackluster The two components of this compound word—*lack* and *luster*—literally convey this word's sense: without shine or brilliance. Now recall **lackluster's** extended meanings, including *uncreative*, *unoriginal*, and so on.

prosaic Imagine a "**prosaic** mosaic"—all in one dull shade of tile: all gray or all black, for example. Do not confuse **prosaic** with *prose*, which means nonrhythmic speechlike writing that is *not* poetry.

MATCHING

Match the vocabulary words in Column A with *one or more* of their defining characteristics appearing in Column B.

Column A

1. lackluster
2. prosaic
3. cliché
4. vapid
5. banal
6. platitude

Column B

a. a trite saying; banality

b. without zest or flavor

c. without brilliance or originality

d. unoriginal

e. overused expression

f. very boring, drawn out

SENTENCE COMPLETION

Remember: Answer choices can be the lesson words themselves, or words that appear in definitions or Memory Tips. Select a word form and part of speech that fit correctly within the sentence.

1. The supervisor's suggestions to the presenter are both _____ and humdrum, completely lacking excitement and interest.
   (derived, platitudes, insipid, triteness, hack)

2. "Your story about The Three Little Pythons sounds familiar and _____, as if I have heard this tale before," remarked Mr. Johnson as he addressed the wide-eyed creative writer.
   (derivative, tritest, platitude, mundane, cliché)

3. When nothing is new under the sun, the days seem long, dull, and _____.
   (hackneyed, lackluster, platitude, trite, cliché)

4. Speaking in _____, Janice put her audience to sleep as she droned on and on, stringing together one overused expression after another.
   (prosaic, derivative, banal, vapid, clichés)

5. _____ screenplays will never make it in Hollywood because freshness and novelty will invariably be preferred over staleness.
   (Banal, Platitude, Prosaic, Overused, Derivative)

WORDS IN CONTEXT

Based on the context in which each **bold** word is used, identify the word usage of each sentence as either C (Correct) or I (Incorrect).

1. A **vapid** story is something new under the sun.

2. "As white as snow" is not an example of a **banality**.

3. **Cliché** phrasing substantially bolsters the emotional impact of poetry.

4. An expression that "rings a bell" is likely to be considered **hackneyed**.

5. **Trite** essay titles are likely to grab a reader's attention.

Lesson 5

MAKING THINGS BETTER
Words Relating to Lessening Pain, Tension, or Conflict

allay alleviate ameliorate appease assuage conciliate mediate mitigate mollify pacify placate quell

---

allay (uh-LAY) *vb.* to lessen fear; to calm; to relieve pain

- An SAT prep course can **allay** the anxiety of some students, but can heighten tension for others.

  The recorded sound of waterfalls and breaking waves is said to **allay** stress.

  In order to **allay** Allen's worries about his grade in chemistry, Ms. Petrie told him to expect at least an A-minus.

alleviate (uh-LEE-vee-ate) *vb.* to lessen pain or discomfort

- Grandma takes pills to **alleviate** her arthritic pain.

- To **alleviate** overcrowding, the school administration proposes running two class schedules, one early and one late.

  A long soak in a hot tub can **alleviate** the tensions of the day.

ameliorate (uh-MEEL-yuh-rate) *vb.* to make better; to lessen pain, difficulty, or tension

  Marv takes time every day to **ameliorate** the stress of school and work; he takes walks, jogs, gets a massage, or listens to the Grateful Dead.

- The doctor prescribed a new ointment to **ameliorate** the rash on my legs.

- Side curtain airbags **ameliorate** some of my anxiety about driving a small car.

appease (uh-PEEZ) *vb.* to make tranquil or quiet, especially by giving into another's demands; to pacify

Albert comes to French class late most days. Yesterday he tried to **appease** his teacher by bringing her a burrito and a soda.

Madame Goldbrick was amused but not **appeased**, so Albert's grade suffered.

What did Albert do to **appease** his parents? He offered to cook them a gourmet dinner.

assuage (uh-SWAYJ) *vb.* to alleviate; to lessen pain or conflict; pacify

If you bake yourself in the sun, try aloe vera gel to **assuage** the pain of sunburn.

Listening to my tale of woe may help to **assuage** your own troubles.

To help Hildy **assuage** her anger, Tom sat her down and let her vent for a while.

conciliate (kuhn-SIH-lee-ate) *vb.* to win a person over through special considerations or persuasive methods; reconcile

Hoping to end the argument, Judd offered a **conciliatory** handshake to his adversary.

To ease the tensions between the two countries, the prime minister made a **conciliatory** speech on TV.

He toned down the harsh language with some **conciliatory** words such as "sorry" and "please."

mediate (MEE-dee-ate) *vb.* to act as a go-between in settling conflicts or disputes between people or opposing sides

Hal is impartial. That is why he's a good man to **mediate** between the two gangs.

Unless we get a **mediator** who can bring the sides together, the strike won't end until next Christmas.

To be an effective **mediator**, it helps to have experience in resolving conflicts.

mitigate (MIH-tuh-gate) *vb.* to make or become less severe; to lessen pain or damage

A sudden shift in the wind **mitigated** the intensity of the storm.

To **mitigate** the pain in her sore throat, Ellie drank a cup of mint tea with honey.

Ms. Walsh **mitigated** her students' worries about the SAT by holding a review class after school.

mollify (MOL-uh-fie) *vb.* to pacify, soothe, or appease; to make less severe or violent

Jay **mollified** his mother by bringing home all A's on his report card.

I tried to comfort her with hugs, but she wouldn't be **mollified** so easily.

Not even the offer of a free ticket could **mollify** Greg's anger after the airline lost his suitcase.

pacify (PA-suh-fie) *vb.* to calm; to make peaceful; to restore to a tranquil state

After wrecking the family car, Maura tried to **pacify** her parents with a bouquet of daisies.

Mother **pacified** her crying baby by rubbing his tummy.

The unruly crowd refused to be **pacified** by speeches promising better days in the future.

placate (PLAY-kate) *vb.* to make calm; to soothe

What can be done to **placate** impatient drivers caught in a traffic jam?

Don't try to **placate** me by telling me you'll change in the future. Change now!

The restaurant tried to **placate** us with free appetizers after a one-hour wait for a table.

quell (KWEL) *vb.* to pacify; to subdue; to quiet down

Having been tipped off, the police managed to **quell** the disturbance.

Shouting "Quiet!" failed to **quell** the noise in the auditorium.

A nightlight helped to **quell** the baby's fear of the dark.

MEMORY TIPS

Use these mnemonics (memory devices) to boost your vocabulary. Make up your own memory clues for words in this lesson that are personally challenging. Add these tips—and your own—to your Vocabulary Notebook. Remember, vocabulary building is key to increasing your score on the verbal SAT.

Notice that both mnemonics below use a technique called "Letter Clusters." As the following examples illustrate, Letter Clusters are naturally occurring groups of letters within the vocabulary word that offer hints to the word's meaning.

alleviate Let the first five letters, *allev*, rhyme with *relieve*, which is a condensed definition of **alleviate**.

appease Let the last five letters, *pease*, remind you of *peace*. Link that to the overall meaning of this word—to make peaceful.

assuage Have you ever heard of a slant rhyme? Slant rhymes are imperfect rhymes, whereby the words sound similar—but not exactly the same. One of my favorite memory tips is using a slant rhyme between *assuage* and *massage*. As you know, massage is often used to alleviate tension. Can you see how the meaning of massage relates to your vocabulary word **assuage**?

MATCHING

Match the vocabulary words in Column A with *one or more* of their defining characteristics appearing in Column B.

Column A

1. conciliate
2. mitigate
3. pacify
4. quell
5. alleviate

Column B

a. to make calm
b. to lessen fear and anxiety
c. to soothe
d. to make quiet; to settle down
e. to win someone over

SENTENCE COMPLETION

Remember: Answer choices can be the lesson words themselves, or words that appear in definitions or Memory Tips. Select a word form and part of speech that fit correctly within the sentence.

1. A natural-born peacemaker among her friends and family, Laila makes a talented _____ in the business world as well.
   (mitigator, allay, quell, pacified, mediator)

2. When my stomach is upset, nothing _____ my discomfort as much as a bowl of warm, homemade minestrone soup, sprinkled with lemon zest.
   (alleviates, pacifies, conciliates, mediates, appeases)

3. A simple, sincere "I'm sorry" is often all it takes to _____ with another, even after a long-standing disagreement.
   (allay, mitigate, pacify, quell, conciliate)

4. Tears subsided and happy voices sounded once mother decided to _____ the feud between her son and daughter by actively sympathizing with each child's side of the story, no matter how divergent their tales were.
   (pacifier, appease, conciliate, mitigate, allay)

5. A soft nightlight is one way to _____ nighttime fears and erase spooky visions of monsters under the bed.
   (mollify, conciliate, mediate, placate, allaying)

WORDS IN CONTEXT

Based on the context in which each **bold** word is used, identify the word usage of each sentence as either C (Correct) or I (Incorrect).

1. To **quell** a tumultuous situation, one must first question those involved.

2. For some, listening to the rhythms of waterfalls can help **assuage** strain and anxiety.

3. Once several burdens were lessened, Jessica's anxiety was **alleviated**.

4. The agitators tried to **mollify** the stressed-out shoppers.

5. How can adults be expected to remember how our testing anxieties were best **pacified** by our parents and teachers?

Review Exercises / Lessons 1–5

VOCABULARY-IN-CONTEXT PARAGRAPH

The paragraph below primarily features words that appear in vocabulary lessons 1–5. For added reinforcement, additional vocabulary words from other lessons may appear in the paragraph. In those cases, the lesson number in which those words appear is indicated within parentheses. In light of the context, the words' meanings should be clear. If you are uncertain about particular meanings, however, take a moment to review the word's definition and illustrative sentences, as provided within the referenced lessons.

Lessons 1–5: Character Portrait

Known for her withdrawn demeanor and *reticence*, the *narcissistic* young girl was immersed in a world of her own. She cared not about the frenetic activity or *adversity* (Lesson 10) experienced by those in her midst. *Aloof* (Lesson 13), she tried neither to *mitigate* the tension with supportive *eloquence* nor to *placate* the people involved with helping hands. Peoples' difficulties were *lackluster*; the advice she might offer consisted largely of uninspired *hackneyed* expressions and *platitudes*: "It'll all work out" or "Everything will be okay." After delivering such *trite* remarks, she'd *swagger* off, absorbed in her very own world.

NAME THAT CLUSTER

To the left of the groups of words, put the Roman numeral that corresponds with these theme (or cluster) titles:

Words Relating to . . .

   I. Feeling Superior
  II. Unoriginal, Dull, Played Out
 III. Lessening Pain, Tension, or Conflict
 IV. Using Few Words or Being Quiet
  V. Speaking

Cluster Title _____   1. loquacious, garrulous, rant, prattle, voluble

Cluster Title _____   2. assuage, ameliorate, quell, placate, alleviate

Cluster Title _____   3. hackneyed, trite, mundane, derivative, banal

Cluster Title _____   4. haughty, braggart, swagger, insolent, disdainful

Cluster Title _____   5. taciturn, terse, laconic, pithy, quiescent

---

SENTENCE COMPLETION

Note: On the new SAT (March 2016 and forward), multiple-choice sentence completion questions have been eliminated. However, sentence completion questions remain in this book as a vocabulary-strengthening exercise. Make flashcards for the words that are unknown or unfamiliar to you.

Read the sentence through carefully. Then from the five vocabulary words given in parentheses, circle the word that fits *best*.

1. Sitting alone and speaking to no one, the woman was an example of _____.
   (turpitude, reticence, meandering, analogy, mutiny)

2. It is _____ to think that every individual enjoys your company.
   (egregious, unkind, willful, presumptuous, critical)

3. One favorite object of the _____ is a hand-held mirror in which to gaze adoringly.
   (derivative, bizarre, grandiloquence, egoist, sailor)

4. Your _____ poetry has no chance of winning first prize in the creative writing contest.
   (vapid, haughty, idyllic, penurious, shrewd)

5. Because you have more than 150 thank-you notes to write, I recommend that you make them _____.
   (savvy, rude, meritorious, concise, swaggering)

6. Despite Hank's efforts to _____ the tension between his friends, the bitter feelings could not be _____.
pacify...swaggered
prattle...banal
assuage...rambled
mitigate...alleviated
vapid...hackneyed

7. Tess's _____ reply contradicted her habitual, _____ self.
placating...derivative
lackluster...contemptuous
laconic...voluble
mollified...trite
cliché...haughty

8. Unlike the powerful and tumultuous waters of the Pacific Ocean, where it meets the Sea of Cortez, the waters found at small, nearby beaches and coves are more _____.
(reserved, pacified, tacit, quelled, quiescent)

9. Ms. Fine enthusiastically inquired about her son's day at school, but he replied with a _____ "pretty good."
(acquiescent, complacent, terse, pithy, diffuse)

10. Newspaper headlines leave little room for elaboration; they are short and _____.
(concise, reticent, hackneyed, disdainful, prattling)

ONE DOESN'T BELONG

Three of the words in each grouping relate to each other somehow. Cross off the one word that does not belong with the others. For a challenge, write the word that does not belong on the line below, and try your best to define that word. *Note:* Some of the words have been taken from definitions or exercises that appear within the lessons.

1. pretentious   arrogant   supercilious   garrulous

_____ means _____

2. conciliate   assuage   swagger   mollify

_____ means _____

3. voluble   taciturn   loquacious   verbose

_____ means _____

4. allay   vapid   insipid   platitude

_____ means _____

5. concise   palliate   succinct   pithy

_____ means _____

Lesson 6

THE CONVIVIAL CLUSTER
Words Relating to Friendly and Agreeable

affable amiable amicable congenial convivial cordial gregarious jocular levity

---

affable (AF-uh-bul) *adj.* easy to talk to; easy to approach, friendly; kind; amiable

Affable baseball players willingly sign autographs for the fans; the unfriendly ones refuse.

It's fun to talk with Lisa because she's so **affable** and upbeat.

Don's friendly grin conveys his **affable** personality.

amiable (AY-mee-uh-bul) *adj.* friendly, kind

Amiable Amy says only the kindest things about others; she doesn't understand the meaning of "nasty."

Keith is patient, friendly, and kind—an altogether **amiable** person.

Miss Crabtree frowns and growls a lot. She's a little short on **amiability**.

amicable (A-mih-kuh-bul) *adj.* showing goodwill; peaceable

The conflict came to an **amicable** end when the adversaries finally shook hands.

The **amicable** negotiations ended when the parties began to insult each other.

Blockbuster Video has **amicable** employees. They don't even give you a hard time when you forget to rewind the tape.

congenial (kun-JEE-nee-yul) *adj.* compatible; having kindred needs or tastes; sympathetic

Mr. and Mrs. Evans are a **congenial** couple. They share a passion for antiques and surfboarding.

Sherry won the Miss **Congeniality** award for being the most friendly, considerate, and affable contestant in the pageant.

What a **congenial** place this is! I always feel welcome here.

convivial (kun-VIV-yuhl) *adj.* sociable, outgoing in a festive way, especially when pertaining to eating and drinking; fond of good company

A **convivial** crowd will be coming to the party; therefore, it should be fun.

Jake is a party animal, one of the most **convivial** guys I know.

Bad food and bad music put everyone in a bad mood. Let's try to make the next dance more **convivial**.

cordial (CORE-juhl) *adj.* warm and friendly; amiable

With a **cordial** welcome, Harry made everyone feel glad to be at the meeting.

The **cordial** remarks of my guests convinced me that the party was a success.

I spend all day answering the same questions over and over, but I still try to be **cordial** to every customer.

gregarious (gri-GEHR-ee-us) *adj.* sociable, outgoing

I hope that Trudy soon emerges from her shell and becomes more **gregarious**.

As a child Timmy was quiet, but as a teenager he's **gregarious**.

The **gregarious** crowd kept the place buzzing all evening.

jocular (JAH-kyuh-lur) *adj.* liking to be with people, joke around with them and have fun

Jay Leno's **jocular** personality makes him the perfect host for *The Tonight Show*.

Samantha is a funny person, but she's somber compared to her **jocular** sister.

There's nothing like a few **jocular** students to enliven a dull class.

levity (LEH-vuh-tee) *n.* lightheartedness; gaiety; carefree disposition, particularly when not appropriate

- "Cheating is a serious issue," said the exam proctor. "There's no room for **levity** in this discussion."

  There was plenty of loud laughter. In fact, you could hear the **levity** in the room from the other end of the corridor.

  A little **levity** is needed to lighten up this depressing class.

MEMORY TIPS

Use these mnemonics (memory devices) to boost your vocabulary. Make up your own memory clues for words in this lesson that are personally challenging. Add these tips—and your own—to your Vocabulary Notebook. Remember, a bigger vocabulary typically means a bigger SAT score.

amicus In Latin, **amicus** means "friend." See how the stem of this Latin word appears in several words relating to friendly: **amiable**, **amicable**. *Ami-* also appears in **amity**, which means "friendship." Consider these SAT antonyms: **amity** ↔ **enmity**.

gregarious Learning the root word is key to remembering this word. As a Latin root, "gregis" means *herd* or *group*. Someone **gregarious** likes to be around herds of people or groups; therefore, **gregarious** means sociable.

jocular Simply, let *joc* remind you of *joking*. Now picture someone joking around, being friendly, and having fun—the personification of **jocular**! Or, try this: Picture a **jocular** jock, laughing and smiling while effortlessly twirling a basketball on his middle finger!

levity Contradictions and opposites tend to stick in our memory. So, if you know that *gravity* means "seriousness," remember its antithesis, or opposite, **levity**. Here's the visual: **levity** ↔ **gravity**.

Remember, the best memory clues are the ones that work for *you*.

MATCHING

Match the vocabulary words in Column A with *one or more* of their defining characteristics appearing in Column B.

Column A

1. affable
2. jocular
3. gregarious
4. levity
5. convivial

Column B

a. kind and friendly
b. extroverted
c. lightheartedness, humor
d. liking to joke around, have fun
e. enjoying food and good company

SENTENCE COMPLETION

Remember: Answer choices can be the lesson words themselves, or words that appear in definitions or Memory Tips. Select a word form and part of speech that fit correctly within the sentence.

1. The department chair advised Miss Prim to replace her serious, stiff teaching style with a (an) _____ approach that would engage and enliven her students—even spark them to laugh occasionally—so that they would have more fun while learning.
   (levity, affable, compatible, convivial, jocular)

2. _____ and pleasant conversation is always welcome in this house; save the sarcasm and complaints for elsewhere.
   (Gregarious, Congenial, Cordial, Enmity, Gravity)

3. Hands down, he is always the life of the party. With the karaoke mike in one hand and a cocktail frank in the other, it's no wonder they call him _____ Claude!
   (cordial, congenial, convivial, levity, peaceable)

4. If gravity is studying five hours for a precalculus test, then _____ is sinking into the couch and sucking on a Ring Pop while watching *Glee* for the umpteenth time.
   (amity, levity, enmity, affability, jocularity)

5. Students at Middlebury High School can always count on Amanda, kind-spirited and _____, to spread benevolent words about her friends, teachers, and acquaintances.
(affability, congenial, amiable, gregarious, conviviality)

WORDS IN CONTEXT

Based on the context in which each **bold** word is used, identify the word usage of each sentence as either C (Correct) or I (Incorrect).

1. **Gregarious** Gus enjoys, above all else, the peace and calm of being alone.

2. Hilda's steady nodding showed her **cordial** acceptance of our change of plans.

3. **Jocularity** abounds during the holidays, with all the fun and festivity.

4. Saying "please" and "thank you" is a poor example of **cordial** behavior.

5. Many neighbors avoid the elderly woman due to her **affable** personality.

Lesson 7

THE CANTANKEROUS CLUSTER

Words Relating to Quarreling, Fighting, and Bitter Feelings

---

animosity antagonism bellicose belligerent cantankerous captious contentious disputatious polemical predator pugnacious

---

animosity (a-nuh-MAH-suh-tee) *n.* hatred; ill will

So much **animosity** grew between Mark and Mike that they never were buddies again.

Ursula's **animosity** toward Eddie hardened her heart.

Sonya's sarcasm raised the level of **animosity** between her and Liz.

antagonism (an-TA-guh-nih-zum) *n.* hatred or hostility

Stan's mocking and teasing incited **antagonism** among his teammates.

He is tormented by the **antagonism** of his classmates, who ride him unmercifully.

Roy and Charlie used to be pals, but an argument over Millie turned them into **antagonists**.

bellicose (BEH-lih-kose) *adj.* of a quarrelsome nature; eager to fight; warlike; belligerent

The speech was full of **bellicose** threats, suggesting war was at hand.

The **bellicose** coach lost his job after he told his players: "Kill them bums!"

After Richie's nose was broken in a fight, his **bellicose** behavior diminished.

belligerent (buh-LIJ-runt) *adj*. taking part in war or fighting; ready to fight

After two decades of war, the **belligerent** countries made peace.

When told to rewrite her essay, Gertie grew **belligerent** and yelled at her teacher.

Noah's **belligerence** started the fight.

cantankerous (kan-TANG-kuh-rus) *adj*. bad-tempered or irritable; quarrelsome

Cantankerous Timmy is my two-year old brother. He whines a lot and throws his oatmeal all over the kitchen.

Grandma and Grandpa are a **cantankerous** old couple, always fighting and scolding.

When my dad gets up on the wrong side of the bed, he's **cantankerous** the whole day.

captious (CAP-shus) *adj*. made for the sake of quarreling; quibbling

My English teacher, Ms. Carr, quibbles over every word. She criticizes her students' writing with **captious** comments.

Jon used to be laid back and easygoing, but since his parents' divorce he's **captious** about everything.

My supervisor does nothing but bicker with the staff. His **captiousness** forced me to quit my job.

contentious (kun-TEN-shus) *adj*. quarrelsome; belligerent

You can't talk to **contentious** Cal without getting into an argument.

I get along well with my sister, but my brother and I are usually **contentious**.

If you don't stop being **contentious**, no one will want to cooperate with you.

disputatious (dis-pyuh-TAY-shus) *adj*. likely to dispute or argue

Ken loves to argue just for the sake of arguing. With such a **disputatious** personality, he's sure to be a trial lawyer.

I don't want to be **disputatious**, but I think you are completely wrong about Hester's motives.

Hoping to provoke lively class discussions, Mr. Phillips raises controversial issues and assumes a **disputatious** personality.

polemical (puh-LEH-mih-kul) *adj*. inclined to argue or debate; controversial

When Donna disagrees, she doesn't calmly differ with you, but tends to be **polemical**.

Because their feelings ran high, several senators engaged in strong **polemical** exchanges to support their opinions.

The speech was not a reasonable argument against gun control; it was more of a **polemic**.

predator (PREH-duh-tur) *n*. one who takes advantage of another, exploits or feeds on another; a strong adversary or rival

Tonight I'll try to catch the **predator** who raided the henhouse last night and killed my prize rooster.

He's a con man, a known **predator** who cons unsuspecting old folks into trusting him to profitably invest their life savings.

Watch out for **predatory** schemers who'll take your money and run.

pugnacious (puhg-NAY-shus) *adj*. eager to fight; belligerent

Pugnacious Paul, as you might expect, was involved in another schoolyard brawl.

Walter and Willa are a **pugnacious** pair, always squabbling and fighting.

Beware of **pugnacious** salesmen who'll bully you into buying things you don't need.

MEMORY TIPS

Use these mnemonics (memory devices) to boost your vocabulary. Make up your own memory clues for words in this lesson that are personally challenging. Add these catchy tips—and your own—to your Vocabulary Notebook. Remember, vocabulary building is key to increasing your score on the verbal SAT.

antagonism From your English class discussions, you most likely already know who an *antagonist* is. He or she is the person who rivals the novel's main character, or protagonist. Since these two characters are in opposition, there is a feeling of **antagonism** between them. Now, simply put, remember that a story's antagonist is likely to feel a sense of **antagonism** (hostility, aversion) toward the rival protagonist.

bellicose, belligerent "Belli" is a Latin root for war. By memorizing this word root, you can help yourself learn two words for the price of one root!

cantankerous Have you ever had a canker sore in your mouth? If so, you know how uncomfortable, even painful, one can be. If Casey had a canker sore in his mouth, then he might be **cantankerous** (bad-tempered, quarrelsome). Think of "canker sore" when you see **cantankerous**.

contentious Even though *content* means happy, **contentious** means quarrelsome. Remember this word because of its unexpected twist!

pugnacious Remember the schoolyard bully? Create a picture in your mind's eye of the bully as *pug*-nosed and ruddy-faced. Can you see the bully? Now, link *pug* from pug-nosed to the *pug* in the vocabulary word **pugnacious** (ready to fight).

MATCHING

Match the vocabulary words in Column A with *one or more* of their defining characteristics appearing in Column B.

Column A	Column B
1. polemical	a. ready to fight
2. contentious	b. liking to argue
3. predator	c. one who takes advantage of others
4. disputatious	d. controversial
5. belligerent	e. bad-tempered

SENTENCE COMPLETION

Remember: Answer choices can be the lesson words themselves, or words that appear in definitions or Memory Tips. Select a word form and part of speech that fit correctly within the sentence.

1. "Lose your _____ tone," Miranda firmly remarked; "otherwise I am unwilling to continue this confrontational conversation with you."
(antagonist, contentious, belligerence, predatory, aversion)

2. Opportunistic Pete practices one _____ move after another; he's either cheating, scheming, or planning his next lie.
(polemical, disputatious, bellicose, cantankerous, predatory)

3. In politics, diplomacy and _____ are on extreme opposite ends of the relationship continuum that exists between nations.
(belligerence, polemics, captious, predator, quibbling)

4. First a disgruntled customer, then an uncooperative delivery truck driver—wherever salesclerk Jared turned, a red-eyed _____ was there to glare at him in the face.
(disputatious, predator, antagonist, belligerent, cantankerous)

5. "Please, just this once," Julie pleaded, "agree with what I am saying, and stop being so difficult and _____."
(animosity, disputatious, contention, polemic, predatory)

WORDS IN CONTEXT

Based on the context in which each **bold** word is used, identify the word usage of each sentence as either C (Correct) or I (Incorrect).

1. Dean White's **antagonistic** remarks inspired gratitude and warmth in the student body of Caliope High.

2. However content one may be, one is likely to become **contentious** every once in a while.

3. **Pugnacious** tendencies aside, Leo was best characterized as tolerant and agreeable.

4. Complaining shrilly and demanding more than was deserved, the irritable restaurant patron behaved **antagonistically**.

5. Patty and Pete are **predatory** partners; they accommodate each other's needs so that each benefits from a feeling of well-being.

SPENDING AND OVERSPENDING

Words Relating to Generosity in Spending Money and Showing Concern for Others

altruistic benevolent largess lavish magnanimous
munificent philanthropic prodigal profligate squander

---

altruistic (al-troo-ISS-tik) *adj.* showing an unselfish concern for others

Donna is a supreme example of **altruism**. She leads youth groups, delivers meals to the homebound, and volunteers at the local hospital.

Altruistic Al never thinks of himself; he devotes all his time to helping others.

Barbara's motives were not altogether **altruistic**. She had much to gain from serving as the head of the school's blood drive.

benevolent (buh-NEV-lunt) *adj.* giving freely and easily to others; charitable; kind

Ready to help anyone at any time, Tina is about the most **benevolent** person I know.

A **benevolent** streak in Dr. Little compelled him to give up his lucrative practice in New York and help fight AIDS in Africa.

No one has helped our library as much as you have. Your **benevolence** is greatly appreciated.

largess (lar-ZHEHS) *n.* generous giving (also spelled *largesse*)

Sam is famous for his **largess**. Knowing Sam is a big tipper, the staff at his favorite hotel is always glad to see him.

To survive on the street, beggars often depend on the **largess** of passersby.

The **largess** of their alumni has enabled many colleges to offer scholarships to deserving students.

lavish (LA-vish) *adj.* generous in giving to others or in spending money

For her sixteenth birthday, Sarah received **lavish** gifts, including a trip to Hawaii and a BMW convertible.

Despite a modest income, the McTaveys make **lavish** donations to their church.

Because Rod spent **lavishly** on scuba diving gear and hot-air ballooning, he couldn't afford to pay his phone bill.

magnanimous (mag-NA-nuh-mus) *adj.* generous in overlooking insult or injury by others; rising above pettiness

After the attempt on his life, the Pope **magnanimously** forgave the man who shot him.

It's amazing that a man as selfish as James has the nerve to call himself **magnanimous**.

Mr. Appel **magnanimously** offered full college scholarships to any children in the sixth grade who stayed in school and graduated from high school.

munificent (myoo-NIH-fuh-sunt) *adj.* very generous

It's easy to be **munificent** when you already have more of everything than you'll ever want or need.

In a **munificent** act of friendship, Eileen gave up her tickets to the concert so that Emily could go with her new boyfriend.

Her **munificence** was evident in the costly gifts she gave to her family and friends.

philanthropic (fih-lun-THRAH-pik) *adj.* showing a desire to help others by giving gifts; charitable; humane

My mother works for a **philanthropic** organization that disburses funds to needy hospitals.

Bill Gates donates millions of dollars a year to education, medical research, and other **philanthropic** causes.

By definition, a **philanthropist** helps those in need.

prodigal (PRAH-dih-gul) *adj.* wasteful; lavish

Marcia's **prodigal** spending at the mall used up the money she'd been saving for college. Next time, maybe she'll spend more thoughtfully.

Unable to control his expenses, Krups spent **prodigally** until he was broke.

The maxim "A penny saved is a penny earned" means nothing to **prodigals** like Hillary and Hal.

profligate (PRAH-fluh-git) *adj.* wasteful; careless, even reckless, with spending money; extravagant

His **profligate** shopping and dining habits irritate the girl who spends her money wisely and saves up for a rainy day.

Profligate in her spending, Brittany had many unused clothing items hanging with tags in her closet.

Profligate individuals rarely shop the sales racks or use store coupons.

squander (SKWAN-dur) *vb.* to spend money (or time) in a wasteful, uncaring fashion

Jimmy **squandered** a perfectly good day, aimlessly watching TV from dawn to dusk.

"Don't **squander** your paycheck on designer clothes," advised Aunt Rose. "Spend it on something useful."

Because he wasn't thinking straight at the time, Roy **squandered** his chance for a great summer job in Washington, D.C.

MEMORY TIPS

Use these mnemonics (memory devices) to boost your vocabulary. Make up your own memory clues for words in this lesson that are personally challenging. Add these tips—and your own—to your Vocabulary Notebook. Remember, vocabulary building is key to increasing your score on the verbal SAT.

benevolent As a frequently-used prefix, *bene-* means *good.* Remember that simple word root, and the sense of *goodwill* will come through when you see the word **benevolent.** Additional words that start with the prefix *bene-* include: benediction (a blessing), benefactor (a do-gooder), and beneficial (helpful).

largess If you're a visual learner (most of us are), this memory tip will appeal to you. Because **largess** means generous giving, let this word picture work for you: **LARGE$$**. Each S becomes a dollar sign to symbolize the giving nature of this word. "*Large* giving," or **largess**, does not have to exclusively mean giving money. Largess can also deal with giving of your time or giving other gifts.

magnanimous Once again, word roots are your memory clues. "Magna" means *big*, and "animus" means *spirit*. Link these two roots together, and you get *big-spirited*, the sense of generosity behind **magnanimous**.

MATCHING

Match the vocabulary words in Column A with *one or more* of their defining characteristics appearing in Column B.

Column A	Column B
1. lavish	a. big-spirited when it comes to giving
2. prodigal	b. to spend too freely
3. squander	c. showing concern for others
4. altruistic	d. goodwill
5. benevolent	e. wasteful

SENTENCE COMPLETION

Remember: *Answer choices can be the lesson words themselves, or words that appear in definitions or Memory Tips. Select a word form and part of speech that fit correctly within the sentence.*

1. _____ Bernadette always strives to be kindly toward others, without looking for praise, payback, or recognition.
   (Lavish, Squandering, Prodigal, Largess, Benevolent)

2. _____ Janice is truly magnificent, especially when it comes to giving of her time, her help, and her dreamy homemade desserts.
   (Prodigal, Humane, Lavishly, Squandering, Munificent)

3. With a giving spirit, Donald practices _____ each month by giving a portion of his earnings to his three favorite charities. (altruistic, largess, prodigality, lavish, benediction)

4. Although Rori preached _____ to whomever she could, she was one of the most self-indulgent and egocentric individuals. (squander, benefactor, prodigally, altruism, benevolently)

5. The epitome of _____, Luke sought to give of his time, resources, and encouragement whenever the opportunity arose. (squanderer, lavishness, magnanimity, munificent, prodigal)

WORDS IN CONTEXT

Based on the context in which each **bold** word is used, identify the word usage of each sentence as either C (Correct) or I (Incorrect).

1. In order to teach her nephew how to **squander** his nickels and pennies, Aunt Laura bought Trevor a blue piggy bank.

2. Receiving gifts is Jane's delight, for hers is an **altruistic** soul.

3. **Benevolent** gestures are meant to better the lives of others.

4. Respected for her consistent **magnanimity**, Dina was recognized as "Do-Gooder of the Year."

5. **Prodigal** spending habits are unlikely to pay off in the long run.

<table>
<tr><td>

Lesson 9

</td><td>

PENNY-PINCHING TIGHTWAD?

Words Relating to Cheapness or Care with Spending Money

</td></tr>
</table>

austere avaricious frugal mercenary miserly parsimonious penurious thrifty

---

austere (aw-STEER) *adj.* having great economy; showing self-control when it comes to foregoing luxuries and frills; stern in manner or appearance

The poet had lived an **austere** life, foregoing all luxuries and creature comforts.

* Early in their marriage, my parents lived on an **austere** budget that allowed them to buy nothing beyond the bare essentials.

To save money on our trip, we stayed in **austere** little motels that provided little more than a bed and a shower.

avaricious (a-vuh-RIH-shus) *adj.* greedy

* The mayor's **avaricious** nature caused him to embezzle funds from the city's coffers.

She was young and beautiful; he was old but very rich. Rumors said that her **avaricious** tendency drove her to marry him.

Avarice motivates many people to cheat on their income tax.

frugal (FROO-gul) *adj.* careful with money; thrifty; not prodigal or wasteful

As a **frugal** carpenter, Emil finds a use for every scrap of wood. Nothing goes to waste in Emil's shop.

* Surprisingly, they were **frugal** at breakfast, but they spared no expense at dinner.

Frugality kept the old woman from spending a penny on anything she didn't absolutely need.

mercenary (MUR-suh-nehr-ee) *adj.* greedy for self-gain; thinking only of money-making

The **mercenary** owner of the leather store was too money-hungry to ever hold a sale.

He cared little about the quality of his merchandise. As a **mercenary**, he focused only on the size of his profit.

What appeared at first to be **mercenary** turned out to be a totally unselfish endeavor.

miserly (MY-zur-lee) *adj.* careful with how money is spent; thrifty

To lose weight, I eat a **miserly** breakfast: one prune and a cup of fat-free milk.

Too **miserly** to spend a dollar, she'd rather walk than take the crosstown bus.

I never realized what a **miser** Eric was until he refused to give me a sip from his water bottle when we were hiking together.

parsimonious (par-suh-MOE-nee-us) *adj.* overly thrifty or miserly

Gramps is **parsimonious** with his words. Sometimes he doesn't speak for days.

Parsimonious Paul never buys anything unless it's on sale.

He's generous to his family, but to outsiders he is the epitome of **parsimony**.

penurious (puh-NOOR-ee-us) *adj.* stingy; relating to great poverty, destitution

His **penurious** childhood taught my father the value of every penny.

Stop being so **penurious** and give a few dollars to help the homeless.

The **penury** of the family was made apparent by the small cup of soup and crust of bread that Ma served for dinner.

thrifty (THRIF-tee) *adj.* showing care with how money and resources are spent or used

Being **thrifty** is one thing, but being downright cheap is another.

Be **thrifty** for the next few months, and you'll save enough for a new iPhone.

Mama practiced **thrift** by dressing the kids in hand-me-downs rather than in new clothes.

MEMORY TIPS

Use these mnemonics (memory devices) to boost your vocabulary. Make up your own memory clues for words in this lesson that are personally challenging. Add these tips—and your own—to your Vocabulary Notebook. Remember, vocabulary building is key to increasing your score on the verbal SAT.

austere Link the letter cluster *ster* to the *ster* in <u>ster</u>n. Also, let "severe," which is a synonym for this vocabulary word, be a rhyming definition for **austere**. The noun form is **austerity**. You can link *austerity* to *severity* as a rhyming synonym pair. Think in terms of severity/austerity when it comes to cutting back on spending, for example.

mercenary Think *me!* when you see this word. One who is **mercenary** thinks primarily of self-gain (*me!*). In your Vocabulary Notebook, write MErcenary with a highlighted capital ME to emphasize this clue for *greedy*.

parsimonious How this word sounds is key to this mnemonic. Think of someone taking *moni* (money) and putting it in her *pars* (purse). See this simple act as a symbol of cheapness, the basic meaning of **parsimonious**.

penurious Because "penniless" sounds similar to **penurious**, let "penniless" be a simple, rhyming definition for this word. The noun form of this word, **penury**, means "poverty." **Penury** (*n.*) and "poverty" also sound alike, don't they? They both have three syllables, and they start and end with the same letters, p.....y.

thrifty Unlike miserly, **thrifty** has a positive connotation. To remind you that it's often beneficial to be **thrifty**, use this rhyming chant: "It's nifty to be **thrifty**! It's nifty to be **thrifty**! It's nifty to be **thrifty**!" Repeat this chant three times. **Thrift** is the noun form.

MATCHING

Match the vocabulary words in Column A with *one or more* of their defining characteristics appearing in Column B.

Column A

1. austere
2. avarice
3. penurious
4. frugal
5. miser

Column B

a. one who hoards money for himself
b. economizing
c. penniless
d. greed
e. restricted with spending

SENTENCE COMPLETION

Remember: Answer choices can be the lesson words themselves, or words that appear in definitions or Memory Tips. Select a word form and part of speech that fit correctly within the sentence.

1. The knuckles of the _____ old man were perpetually white from strongly clutching his coins, dollars, and prized possessions.
   (penury, parsimony, austere, miserly, frugal)

2. Distressingly, the _____ community was overwrought with one-parent homes, drug peddling, and petty crime, all resulting from destitution.
   (penurious, thrifty, mercenary, austerity, parsimonious)

3. _____ can be an insatiable drive, for sometimes even excessive wealth and material goods is just never enough.
   (Parsimony, Thriftiness, Frugality, Austerity, Avarice)

4. To adopt a more _____ lifestyle, Grant froze his gym membership, said goodbye to his daily mocha latte from Starbucks, and remorsefully asked his cleaning lady if she would be kind enough to come just once a month.
   (penurious, avaricious, austere, mercenary, parsimonious)

5. Using the newspaper comics as wrapping paper and returning soda cans to the grocery store are two ways that a family can practice _____.

(penury, avarice, mercenary, miserly, thrift)

WORDS IN CONTEXT

Based on the context in which each **bold** word is used, identify the word usage of each sentence as either C (Correct) or I (Incorrect).

1. "Your untidy room proves that you are **miserly!**" scolded older sister.

2. **Parsimony** portends the increasing selfishness of humankind.

3. Using a sheet of paper on only one side is a sign of a **miserly** individual.

4. **Mercenaries** and tightwads are two of a kind.

5. Dishearteningly, **penurious** living conditions can contribute to despair and ill will on the part of the dwellers.

MOLE HILLS OR MOUNTAINS?

Words Relating to Problems, Puzzlements, and Disasters

adversity conflagration confounding cryptic debacle enigma
labyrinth precarious quagmire quandary turbulence turmoil

adversity (ad-VUR-suh-tee) *n*. great trouble or difficulty

The book tells how he overcame the **adversity** of an impoverished childhood.

The hero faced four years of **adversity** trying to survive on a deserted island.

If you can get through your junior year in high school, you can get through any **adversity** that may come along.

conflagration (kahn-fluh-GRAY-shun) *n*. a huge fire, an inferno

Flames from the **conflagration** lit up the sky for miles around.

The burning of Atlanta is one of the great **conflagration** scenes in movie history.

During the **conflagration** of 1991, 3,000 homes burned to the ground.

confounding (kun-FOUN-ding) *adj*. puzzling; baffling

The world was fascinated by the **confounding** disappearance of Amelia Earhart.

Who ate the strawberries continues to be a **confounding** mystery.

The possible existence of extraterrestrial life has **confounded** scientists for decades.

cryptic (KRIP-tik) *adj.* hidden; hard to understand; mysterious; obscure

We found a **cryptic** message scrawled on the blackboard. No one could figure out its meaning.

The twins used a **cryptic**, incomprehensible language to talk with each other.

The agent left a trail of **cryptic** notes that only the spymaster could decipher.

debacle (dee-BAH-kul) *n.* a failure or breakdown; a collapse that is often nonsensical

For me, physics class was a **debacle**. I understood none of it, failed every test, and finally dropped the course.

The 45–0 score suggests that the game was a **debacle** for the losing side.

The play was a **debacle**. Actors forgot their lines, the set fell down, and the lights blew out halfway through the first act.

enigma (eh-NIG-muh) *n.* a riddle or mystery; a puzzling or baffling matter or person

Isabelle is an **enigma**. I can't figure her out. Her moods change like the wind, and sometimes I haven't the faintest idea what she's talking about.

James acts mysteriously to prevent others from understanding him too well. He prefers to remain an **enigma**.

The **enigmatic** carvings on the ancient Egyptian tomb never have been fully interpreted.

labyrinth (LA-buh-rinth) *n.* a maze from which it is very hard to extricate or free oneself

The basement of our school is a **labyrinth** of tunnels, criss-crossing passageways, and dead ends in which it is easy to lose your way.

The plumbing system in my house is a **labyrinth** of copper pipes that turn and bend every which way.

Applying to college often seems like trying to find your way through a complicated maze or **labyrinth**.

precarious (prih-CARE-ee-us) *adj.* dangerous or risky; uncertain

Bungee jumping is too **precarious** for me; I prefer safer activities like playing chess.

Because Finny's foothold on the tree limb was **precarious**, he fell and broke his leg.

It's **precarious** to apply to only one college because you may not be admitted, and then what?

quagmire (KWAG-my-ur) *n.* a difficult or troubling situation; a swampy ground, bog, mire

A **quagmire** of troubles kept Julia awake at night.

Once Pete freed himself from his **quagmire** of unpaid bills, he began to reorganize his finances.

Unable to avoid the quicksand, Rebecca began sinking into the **quagmire**!

quandary (KWAN-duh-ree) *n.* a dilemma; a confusing or puzzling situation

Walter faced the enviable **quandary** of deciding which of three hot colleges he should attend.

Confronted with the **quandary** of staying home with her new baby or going back to work, my sister chose to return to her job.

Safe Rides has taken the **quandary** out of whether to accept a ride with a driver who's been drinking.

turbulence (TUR-byoo-luns) *n.* great unrest; turmoil or disorder

In September, Mac and Meg were a happy couple. Since Mary came along, their relationship has experienced some **turbulence**.

Migrating whales caused the **turbulence** in the water.

To give the passengers a smooth flight, the pilot steered the plane around the air **turbulence**.

turmoil (TUR-moyl) *n.* a turbulent scenario or situation; tumult

There was **turmoil** in the room because the teacher had lost control of the class.

Gretchen's emotions were in **turmoil** after Jerry unexpectedly broke up with her.

Terry took a long walk in the peaceful woods to escape the **turmoil** in her house. .

MEMORY TIPS

Use these mnemonics (memory devices) to boost your vocabulary. Make up your own memory clues for words in this lesson that are personally challenging. Add these tips—and your own—to your Vocabulary Notebook. Remember, vocabulary building is key to increasing your score on the verbal SAT.

As the following examples show, using your preexisting knowledge is a highly effective way to learn "new" information:

adversity As you might already know, an *adversary* is an opponent or foe. So, think of **adversity** as any situation that presents a problem or difficult situation, just as an adversary does.

confounding Let **confounding** "slant rhyme" with *confusing*.

cryptic Likewise, as you might already know, a *crypt* is a cave. Inside a cave, it's dark. Writing on the wall, for example, is hard to read. You can picture the inside of a cave, right? So, link your familiarity with what a cave is to this vocabulary word, **cryptic** (hidden, obscure, dark).

MATCHING

Match the vocabulary words in Column A with *one or more* of their defining characteristics appearing in Column B.

Column A

1. conflagration
2. adversity
3. precarious
4. quandary
5. cryptic

Column B

a. big trouble
b. a very difficult situation
c. uncertain or risky
d. a huge fire
e. hidden, mysterious

SENTENCE COMPLETION

Remember: Answer choices can be the lesson words themselves, or words that appear in definitions or Memory Tips. Select a word form and part of speech that fit correctly within the sentence.

1. Rather than picturing a ferocious and potentially lethal blaze when you imagine a (an) _____, visualize a scenic bonfire on the beach at night—complete with toasted marshmallows, hot chocolate, and stargazing!
   (debacle, labyrinth, enigma, adversity, conflagration)

2. Even after being in her presence on several social occasions, Heidi remains a (an) _____ because she hardly speaks and gives only brief answers when she is asked questions.
   (adversity, confounding, conflagration, enigma, turmoil)

3. Despite the _____ of her busy afternoons—homework, carpooling, dinner preparation—Annabelle strives to maintain an inner sense of order and calm.
   (labyrinth, turbulence, enigma, cryptic, precariousness)

4. The dormitory seemed like a (an) _____; the bedrooms, hallways, and common living quarters intersected each other in an intricate, maze-like pattern.
   (quandary, enigma, labyrinth, turmoil, quagmire)

5. Despite Michael's proficiency in mathematics, he still finds advanced algebra _____ and attends extra-help sessions two mornings a week.
   (confounding, labyrinthine, turbulent, adversary, quagmire)

WORDS IN CONTEXT

Based on the context in which each **bold** word is used, identify the word usage of each sentence as either C (Correct) or I (Incorrect).

1. **Turmoil** is the manifestation of a tranquil mind.

2. Where there is overcrowding, a **conflagration** is scarcely detectable.

3. How you manage **adversity** tells something about your inner character.

4. **Enigmatic** situations require a great deal of thinking.

5. Conflicting values and backgrounds can contribute to some degree of interpersonal **turmoil**.

Review Exercises / Lessons 6–10

VOCABULARY-IN-CONTEXT PARAGRAPH

The paragraph below primarily features words that appear in vocabulary lessons 6–10. For added reinforcement, additional vocabulary words from other lessons may appear in the paragraph. In those cases, the lesson number in which those words appear is indicated within parentheses. In light of the context, the words' meanings should be clear. If you are uncertain about particular meanings, however, take a moment to review the word's definition and illustrative sentences, as provided within the referenced lessons.

Lessons 6–10: Venezia: The Magical City on Water

Smiling widely as he navigates the *labyrinth* of canals, the *amiable* gondolier speaks frankly and with *candor* (Lesson 31) about the *adversity* facing his birthplace, Venice. Due to the *precarious* situation created by seasonal flooding, many first-floor dwellings and souvenir shops have been boarded up and abandoned. Despite the *enigma* facing his magical city, the *gregarious* gondolier appears *jocular* as he sings the inspiring lyrics of *Volare* (to fly!). Gazing at the Gothic-inspired architecture and the *lavish* sculptures of golden-winged lions and godly warriors, we spot balconies of elaborate ironwork teeming with bright summer blooms.

NAME THAT CLUSTER

To the left of the groups of words, put the Roman numeral that corresponds with these theme (or cluster) titles:

Words Relating to . . .

I. Cheapness or Care with Spending Money
II. Friendly and Agreeable
III. Generosity in Spending Money and Showing Concern for Others
IV. Quarreling, Fighting, and Bitter Feelings
V. Problems, Puzzlements, and Disasters

Cluster Title _____ 1. benevolent, largess, munificent, philanthropic, magnanimity

Cluster Title _____ 2. amicable, amiable, cordial, gregarious, jocular

Cluster Title _____ 3. quandary, adversity, debacle, labyrinth, cryptic

Cluster Title _____ 4. bellicose, antagonistic, captious, contentious, predator

Cluster Title _____ 5. frugal, penurious, thrifty, austere, miserly

---

SENTENCE COMPLETION

Note: On the new SAT (March 2016 and forward), multiple-choice sentence completion questions have been eliminated. However, sentence completion questions remain in this book as a vocabulary-strengthening exercise. Make flashcards for the words that are unknown or unfamiliar to you.

Read the sentence through carefully. Then, from the five vocabulary words given in parentheses, circle the word that fits *best*.

1. "Sweetheart," Mr. Dire said to his wife, "we need to go on a tight budget. In other words, we have to practice some _____ around here."
   (benevolence, amity, austerity, conflagration, debacle)

2. Are you shy around unfamiliar people, or do you consider yourself _____?
   (frugal, antagonistic, turbulent, parsimonious, gregarious)

3. Gwyneth is in such a (an) _____ mood. It's as if she can't wait to bite the head off the next person who opens his mouth!
   (prodigal, altruistic, convivial, thrifty, contentious)

4. Walking along wet, mossy stones in the water is _____; you very well might slip and fall headfirst into the water.
   (parsimonious, precarious, pugnacious, philanthropic, polemical)

5. With her balloon sculpting and bubble blowing, Cleo the Clown created an atmosphere of _____ that every guest enjoyed.
   (antagonism, avarice, animosity, levity, munificence)

6. Although delightfully _____ at public gatherings, enigmatic
   Roger tends to be _____ and uptight when at home.
   captious...bellicose
   cryptic...altruistic
   thrifty...penurious
   amicable...convivial
   jocular...cantankerous

7. The devastating _____ at the Jones' place of business
   seemed to kick off a chain reaction of negative events; one _____
   followed another.
   conflagration...adversity
   debacle...levity
   frugality...antagonism
   largess...altruism
   turmoil...prodigal

8. The _____ comments of his employer assured Jack that
   his boss was satisfied with his job performance and glad that Jack
   had joined the marketing team.
   (labyrinthine, cordial, prodigal, frugal, parsimonious)

9. Despite her _____ personality, Megan is serious about her
   schoolwork and leaves no room for _____ when she has a
   project deadline.
   jocular...levity
   polemical...affability
   cryptic...adversity
   benevolent...altruism
   avaricious...austerity

10. Difficult Donald is already _____ by nature, but lately he
    has become more and more _____.
    congenial...lavish
    captious...magnanimous
    mercenary...turbulent
    disputatious...belligerent
    predatory...prodigal

ONE DOESN'T BELONG

Three of the words in each grouping relate to each other somehow. Cross off the one word that does not belong with the others. For a challenge, write the word that does not belong on the line below, and try your best to define that word. *Note:* Some of the words have been taken from definitions or exercises that appear within the lessons.

1. cantankerous   altruistic   belligerent   antagonistic

   _____ means _____

2. parsimonious   avaricious   conundrum   miserly

   _____ means _____

3. congenial   amenable   convivial   squander

   _____ means _____

4. confounding   mercenary   enigmatic   obscure

   _____ means _____

5. conflagration   magnanimous   philanthropic   charitable

   _____ means _____

Lesson 11

THE BAD, THE VERY BAD, AND THE BADDEST

Words Relating to Harmful or Mean

baneful deleterious detrimental devious impairing iniquitous
malicious nefarious odious ominous pernicious rancorous
virulent

---

baneful (BANE-ful) *adj*. causing ruin; harmful; pernicious

My campus visit was **baneful**. When it was over, I resolved never to go near the place again.

A teacher's **baneful** comments about Becky destroyed her chances of getting into the Honor Society.

Norman's **baneful** remark about Nora's hair ruined the rest of her day.

deleterious (deh-luh-TI-ree-us) *adj*. harmful to one's health or overall welfare; pernicious

PCBs and other harmful pollutants have had a **deleterious** effect on fish in the Hudson River.

Many processed foods contain chemicals and other ingredients that can be **deleterious** to our health.

The arrogance of the new principal had a **deleterious** effect on the morale of the school's staff and students.

detrimental (deh-truh-MEN-tl) *adj*. harmful

To the **detriment** of its Nielsen ratings, *Friends* went on the air at the same time as *Survivor* and lost 25 percent of its audience.

Smoking is known to be **detrimental** to your health.

The trouble Steve caused had a **detrimental** effect on the class' test scores.

devious (DEE-vee-us) *adj.* dishonest or deceptive; tricky

The sly, **devious** fox outwitted the farmer and broke into the henhouse.

Russ is too **devious** to trust with the keys to the equipment closet.

The neighbors could not believe that someone as upright as Hanssen could have been so **devious**.

impairing (im-PAYR-ing) *adj.* harmful, damaging; causing to weaken or lose power or ability

Listening to amped music can be **impairing** to one's auditory sense.

Never allowing her to take the initiative, Leo was **impairing** his girlfriend's ability to become more autonomous.

Taking too many herbal supplements could be **impairing** to one's health.

iniquitous (ih-NIH-kwuh-tus) *adj.* showing a lack of fairness; wicked; vicious

The **iniquitous** referee plainly favored the other team over ours. Every call went against our team.

Income tax cuts that benefit the wealthy will only further the **iniquitous** economic divide between the wealthy and the less fortunate.

Iniquity has no place in a courtroom dedicated to justice.

malicious (muh-LIH-shus) *adj.* intending to hurt or harm another; spiteful

By the show's end, the heckler's insensitive remarks became downright **malicious**.

Malicious gossip did irreparable harm to Hans' reputation.

To save his own neck, Boris **maliciously** accused Beatrice of a crime she didn't commit.

nefarious (nih-FEHR-ee-us) *adj.* very mean and wicked

Of all the rotten scoundrels in the story, Sebastian was the most **nefarious**.

His desire to get a conviction caused the **nefarious** police officer to plant incriminating evidence at the scene of the crime.

Extortion of other kids' lunch money is just one example of Hubert's **nefariousness**.

odious (OH-dee-us) *adj.* loathsome; evil; revolting in a disgusting way

John has the **odious** habit of clipping his toenails in class.

I can't imagine a more **odious** crime than child abuse.

Steerforth was an **odious** character who betrayed his friends and told nothing but lies.

ominous (AH-muh-nus) *adj.* pertaining to an evil omen; foreboding

The dark clouds on the horizon looked **ominous**.

The settlers considered the gravestones alongside the trail **ominous** signs of hardships to come.

Superstitious people regard broken mirrors and black cats as **ominous**.

pernicious (puhr-NI-shus) *adj.* very destructive or harmful, usually in an inconspicuous and relentless way

From the Columbine incident, Ralph got the **pernicious** idea to take a gun to school.

Lady Macbeth planted in her husband's mind the **pernicious** scheme of killing the king and seizing the crown.

Cigarette smoke caused a **pernicious** growth to form in Mr. Down's lungs. Eventually, the malignancy killed him.

rancorous (RANG-kuh-rus) *adj.* deeply hateful or spiteful; malicious

The dinner conversation turned **rancorous** when Louis and Max started to argue.

A **rancorous** feud between two families lies at the heart of *Romeo and Juliet*.

I once felt bitter about her deception, but now I've lost my **rancor**.

virulent (VIHR-uh-lunt) *adj.* extremely poisonous; deadly; full of spiteful hatred

Rattlesnakes are **virulent**; their poison can be fatal.

Although the fumes seem harmless, they are extremely **virulent**.

Bubonic plague was a **virulent** disease that killed millions in medieval Europe.

MEMORY TIPS

Use these mnemonics (memory devices) to boost your vocabulary. Make up your own memory clues for words in this lesson that are personally challenging. Add these tips—and your own—to your Vocabulary Notebook. Remember, memory tips that *you* create are usually the most memorable.

deleterious Imagine something so harmful that it could potentially *delete* its victim. As you can see, this mnemonic uses an existing letter cluster within this vocabulary word.

malicious The prefix *mal-* (meaning *bad*) is helpful to know. Additional SAT words containing this prefix include malevolent (bad-willed), malefactor (an evildoer), and malign (to badmouth, slander).

nefarious Think back to when you were a kid. Do you remember Jafar from the Disney movie *Aladdin*? Jafar was one mean character. Link Jafar to **nefarious**.

ominous Did you know that an *omen* is a sign of something to come in the future—a prophetic sign? (For example, a black cat is an omen of bad luck; a dark cloud is an omen for rainy weather or forthcoming doom.) Well, if you know the word *omen,* you can see how the adjective **ominous** is derived from this simpler word.

Note: Omens can be good or bad. Something **ominous**, however, relates only to something bad.

virulent This chant might help: "**Virulent** virus! **Virulent** virus! **Virulent** virus!" Your preexisting knowledge tells you that a virus is something harmful; simply link that to the meaning of **virulent**.

MATCHING

Match the vocabulary words in Column A with *one or more* of their defining characteristics appearing in Column B.

Column A

1. virulent
2. rancorous
3. nefarious
4. pernicious
5. ominous

Column B

a. potentially deadly
b. portending doom
c. filled with bitter ill will
d. sinister
e. very harmful

SENTENCE COMPLETION

Remember: Answer choices can be the lesson words themselves, or words that appear in definitions or Memory Tips. Select a word form and part of speech that fit correctly within the sentence.

1. To the human lungs, fresh air is a balmy dream; smog, a _____ nightmare.
   (nefarious, rancorous, iniquitous, devious, baneful)

2. Despite myriad programs geared toward societal improvement, still rampant and among the most _____ and _____ crimes are vandalism, assault and battery, and child abduction.
   (odious...nefarious, virulent...pernicious, ominous...detrimental, malevolent...detriment, foreboding...virulence)

3. Although she took a vow of reticence and verbal temperance, Yolanda spread _____, yet true, accounts about her neighbor that eventually drove poor Ms. Jade to move to another town!
   (rancor, bane, ominous, pernicious, devious)

4. Even though Olivia, who tends to exaggerate, buys organic meat and produce, she still worries about hormone-injected meats and pesticide-sprayed fruits that are labeled "organic" even though they are not; as a result, Olivia obsesses about these items being _____ threats to her health.
   (virulent, ominous, malicious, devious, foreboding)

5. According to some nutritionists, a daily vitamin regime could be beneficial to one's health, but overuse of supplements due to a poor diet could be _____ instead.
(iniquitous, nefarious, rancorous, malicious, detrimental)

WORDS IN CONTEXT

Based on the context in which each **bold** word is used, identify the word usage of each sentence as either C (Correct) or I (Incorrect).

1. The **virulent** vapors produced headaches and nausea in those who breathed them in.

2. **Rancor** is born from friendships that have lasted too long.

3. Sneaking out of the house at night and making up stories about post-curfew whereabouts are examples of **devious** conduct.

4. The fictitious character's **nefarious** ways made him the perfect antagonist to the kindly police officer.

5. Filled with anxiety, the young apprentice felt at ease when he saw the **ominous** visions.

YOU SHOULD NOT HAVE DONE THAT!

Words Relating to Criticizing, Disapproving, or Scolding

berate carp castigate censure chastise degrade deprecate
deride disparage impugn rebuff rebuke reprove upbraid

---

berate (bih-RATE) *vb.* to rebuke or scold in a harsh tone

Her parents often **berated** her, but when the scoldings took place in front of her friends, Lulu was humiliated.

The teacher **berated** Jonathan for shouting an obscenity in class.

I don't like to **berate** my children, but this is the last straw. If you come home late again, you can expect a good scolding.

carp (KARP) *vb.* to find fault; to be critical

"**Carping** won't get you anywhere," said the teacher to the nitpicking child. "But expressing your problem-solving ideas will be beneficial to the entire class."

To **carp** is to harp on your discontentment without taking any positive steps toward improving your circumstances.

Sullen and ill-tempered, the **carping** carp stewed at the bottom of the lake, complaining about the cold water, the slimy eels, and the lack of tasty food. (See Memory Tip.)

castigate (KAS-tuh-gate) *vb.* to scold or punish severely

Before **castigating** others about speeding, ask yourself if you always obey the speed limit.

Fearing **castigation**, Myron made sure that he handed in his lab report on time.

The policeman not only issued him a ticket, but **castigated** him for 10 minutes about passing a stopped school bus.

censure (SEN-shur) *vb.* to criticize strongly

A letter of **censure**, criticizing his behavior, was put in his file.

For harassing his secretary, Mr. Packwood was **censured**, but not fired, from his job.

After being publicly **censured**, the woman vowed never to shoplift again.

chastise (chas-TIZE) *vb.* to punish or scold harshly

My parents **chastised** me for putting bubble gum in my little sister's hair.

Being grounded for a month is the worst **chastisement** Loren ever got.

I accept my **chastisement**. It was stupid of me to drive the car across the golf course.

degrade (dih-GRAYD) *vb.* to mock; to lessen the value of someone, something, or an idea; debase; demean

Insecure people **degrade** others in order to make themselves feel more powerful.

"**Degrading** comments are not welcome in this seminar," the professor announced firmly.

One who **degrades** another casts a poor reflection on himself.

deprecate (DE-prih-kayt) *vb.* to show mild disapproval

In class we make only positive comments. Remarks that **deprecate** the work of others are prohibited.

Although I tried very hard this semester, Ms. Bluestone **deprecated** my efforts to improve.

They respond only to praise. **Deprecation** doesn't change their behavior at all.

deride (dih-RIDE) *vb.* to ridicule or make fun of; to scoff at

Do you think that **deriding** others will make you look better? It won't!

Ironically, the same critic who **derided** the play last year praised it this year.

Filled with **derision**, the cocky young man made fun of one person after another.

disparage (dih-SPAR-idj) *vb.* to scorn, ridicule: to sneer at; to belittle or depreciate, lower the estimation of

Do not **disparage** one's willingness to be overtly kind.

Never allowing himself to be a victim of **disparagement**, Niko on no account lets others' snide remarks get to him.

George's egregious behavior **disparages** his entire family.

impugn (im-PYOON) *vb.* to oppose or attack someone or something as false or refutable

The scandal **impugned** the reputation of the judge.

Don't **impugn** my honesty. I never stole a library book.

No one subscribes to that theory anymore. It was **impugned** by new research.

rebuff (rih-BUF) *vb.* to snub; to bluntly refuse

Gigi **rebuffed** Dick's proposal, so Dick asked Margie instead.

Grant's initial request for a raise was **rebuffed**, but he got an increase the second time he asked.

I hoped to make up with him after the argument, but I was **rebuffed**.

rebuke (rih-BYOOK) *vb.* to reprimand or scold sharply

Jill **rebuked** Jack for breaking his crown. "I promise not to do it again," said Jack.

Sarah continued to bite her nails in spite of being **rebuked** time and again.

Charlie won't **rebuke** me for deceiving him. He understands—and given the chance would probably do the same to me.

reprove (rih-PROOV) *vb.* to speak to in a disapproving manner; to scold

Reprovingly, the teacher said, "For the last time, I'm telling you that absence is no excuse for not doing the work."

The teacher **reproved** Sonny for not bringing a note from his parents.

"Stop it!" shouted Mike, "I won't have you **reprove** me for an offense I didn't commit."

upbraid (up-BRAYD) *vb.* to chide; to scold bitterly

> Mr. Judd **upbraided** the class for throwing pencils and paper clips around the room.

> I hate to be scolded for missing a deadline. I could be **upbraided** for many worse things.

> Janet **upbraided** her sister for eavesdropping on her phone calls. "Stay out of my love life," she chided.

MEMORY TIPS

Use these mnemonics (memory devices) to boost your vocabulary. Make up your own memory clues for words in this lesson that are challenging for you. Add these tips—and your own—to your Vocabulary Notebook.

carp Do you know what a carp is? That's right—a freshwater fish! Let's link carp to **carping** by imagining a "carping carp" swimming in a lake. Picture this carp in your mind's eye. What could he be **carping** about—the cloudy water? Too many fish in the pond? Not enough food? Water pollution? Who knows? Picture this carp complaining about and being critical about so many things. He is indeed a "***carping*** *carp.*"

deprecate Do you know what it means for a car (or any asset) to depreciate in value? It means to go down in value. So, link this understanding to **deprecate**. If someone deprecates another's idea, then that person is looking upon the idea with mild disapproval, or *a sense of lesser value*. If this connection works for you, then **deprecate** will no longer be an unknown word for you.

deride Let the letter cluster *rid* kindle *rid*icule, the meaning of this vocabulary word. To **deride** is to ridicule, mock, or make fun of. The noun form *derision* means "ridicule."

impugn Recall *pugn* at the beginning of pugnacious (ready to fight; quarrelsome). Now, link that *pugn* meaning to the verb **impugn**. To impugn is *to oppose* or *attack*; now I'm sure you see the link between this verb and the adjective *pugnacious*. This mnemonic strategy reinforces two words simultaneously.

rebuff, rebuke, reprove Let the *re* at their beginnings link them together in your mind's eye so that you can efficiently learn these three as a group. Learning this trio simultaneously will accelerate your vocabulary building.

MATCHING

Match the vocabulary words in Column A with *one or more* of their defining characteristics appearing in Column B.

Column A

1. deprecate
2. impugn
3. rebuff
4. castigate
5. berate

Column B

a. to criticize harshly
b. to verbally attack
c. to speak to disapprovingly
d. to snub
e. to scold severely

SENTENCE COMPLETION

Remember: *Answer choices can be the lesson words themselves, or words that appear in definitions or Memory Tips. Select a word form and part of speech that fit correctly within the sentence.*

1. Lance is an enigma; at times, I don't know whether to extol him for his helpfulness and flexibility or to _____ him for his cynical and self-serving nature.
   (carp, derision, upbraid, impugn, chastisement)

2. First you _____ me among our closest friends, then you downright _____ me in public—what sort of harsh treatment should I expect next?
   (deprecate...upbraiding, deride...castigate, deprecate...pugnacious, impugn...carp, chastise...rebuff)

3. Instead of complaining about how your parents scold you, get your act together and prove to them that you no longer deserve their _____ for being remiss in your schoolwork and household chores.
   (reproval, carp, censorious, rebuffed, impugning)

4. I felt pushed under the rug when I tried to share my perspective on extracurricular activities with Ava, for my point of view was quickly _____ following her eerie and unsympathetic laugh!
   (carp, upbraided, reproving, rebuffed, berate)

5. Even though Charles' boss bitterly _____ him on account of his reprehensible conduct, the praise he received from his boss earlier in the week remained palpable, continuing to lift his spirits and bolster his self-esteem.
(carped, chastised, castigation, deprecated, upbraid)

WORDS IN CONTEXT

Based on the context in which each **bold** word is used, identify the word usage of each sentence as either C (Correct) or I (Incorrect).

1. After being **rebuffed** by her peers, Harriet felt reassured.

2. The **upbraiding** lifted the spirits of all who were present.

3. The parents eyed their child **deprecatingly**, hoping that their displeasure would persuade the child to change.

4. The center's mission statement was **impugned** as unfair and narrow-minded.

5. The elder's **reproving** tone improved the morale of the hard-working group.

<table>
<tr><td>

Lesson 13

</td><td>

WHO CARES? WHAT'S SO INTERESTING?

Words Relating to Lacking Interest or Emotion

</td></tr>
</table>

> aloof apathetic detached dispassionate impassive indifferent listless nonchalant phlegmatic remote stolid

aloof (uh-LOOF) *adj.* uninterested; showing no concern; emotionally removed or distant

He appears to be **aloof**, but his detachment comes from shyness, not conceit.

The Parkers prefer to stay **aloof** from their neighbors. They didn't even attend the Labor Day block party.

Biff's recent **aloofness** contrasts sharply with his usual gregariousness.

apathetic (a-puh-THEH-tik) *adj.* indifferent; showing no caring, interest, or concern; lacking emotion

The crowd was mostly **apathetic**. They didn't give a hoot who won the game.

"I've heard this school is a hotbed of **apathy**," said the new principal. "Well, I intend to raise school spirit and make kids want to come here each day."

Because of student **apathy**, no one cared enough to collect money to help earthquake victims in India.

detached (dih-TATCHT) *adj.* aloof; indifferent

Jane is **detached** from class activities. She sits passively and never participates in discussions.

Ken seemed to rise above the petty bickering, but he wasn't as **detached** as he appeared.

I'm not getting involved in critiquing the play. I'm just a **detached** observer.

dispassionate (dis-PA-shun-ut) *adj.* lacking an interest in something or someone; unemotional; detached; unconcerned

Although Rishi enjoys chemistry, he is **dispassionate** about the prospect of becoming a chemist, lab researcher, or doctor.

Dispassionate about listening to blaring live music, Miranda rarely attended concerts.

Feeling **dispassionate** about life, Kian wondered if he were suffering from depression.

impassive (im-PA-siv) *adj.* lacking emotion or drive

Jake's **impassive** nature contrasts with Jenny's innate enthusiasm.

Johnny maintained an **impassive** attitude as the rest of the cast complained about the extra rehearsal on Saturday night.

Ten witnesses stood by with **impassive** expressions and did nothing as the killer tormented his victim.

indifferent (in-DI-frunt) *adj.* apathetic; showing little or no concern or care

Vickie is an **indifferent** student. She doesn't study much and doesn't care about her mediocre grades.

I don't want to sound **indifferent**, but it's all the same to me whether I go to college or not.

Your **indifference** really bothers me. I wish you could get excited about the campus visit.

listless (LIST-lis) *adj.* lacking interest in something, usually because of illness, fatigue, or general sadness; spiritless

The heat wave left me **listless**. I just couldn't get up enough energy to study physics.

After discussing the issue, Sheila replied **listlessly**, "Whatever."

She made a **listless** effort to enter the conversation, but she soon gave up.

nonchalant (nahn-chuh-LAHNT) *adj.* casual and indifferent; not showing any great concern or worry about anything

She appears to be **nonchalant** on the court, but she's really trying very hard.

"Completing your application on time is serious business," insisted the counselor. "You mustn't be **nonchalant** about it."

Mark wanted to follow the rules to the letter, but Monica was more **nonchalant** about them.

phlegmatic (fleg-MA-tik) *adj.* hard to get excited or emotional; calm; slow-moving

I feel too **phlegmatic** to go on a bike ride today. Maybe tomorrow I'll be more motivated.

Andrea is too **phlegmatic** to scream and shout about anything.

Although the coach gave the team a pep talk, they played a **phlegmatic** game.

remote (rih-MOTE) *adj.* emotionally distant and disinterested; aloof; uninvolved; distant, far away

Jerry became increasingly **remote** after his parents' divorce. He stopped socializing at school and never returned my phone calls.

Our old cat had a **remote** attitude toward the new kitten, refusing to accept it as part of our household.

In *Cast Away*, the hero found himself alone on a **remote** island for four years.

stolid (STAH-lud) *adj.* lacking emotion or not showing any emotion; stoical

Carrie accepted her fate in **stolid** silence. Whatever emotions she felt remained hidden.

Girls can cry as much as they want. Boys, on the other hand, are supposed to be **stolid**.

Despite the loss of their home in the fire, the Wilsons carried on with **stolid** determination.

MEMORY TIPS

Use these mnemonics (memory devices) to boost your vocabulary. Make up your own memory clues for words in this lesson that are personally challenging. Add these tips—and your own—to your Vocabulary Notebook.

apathetic As a prefix, *a-* means *without*. "Pathos," as a root word, means *feeling*. Link this prefix and root together, and you've got *without feeling*, a workable springboard definition for **apathetic**.

detached Think of **detached** as the antithesis (opposite) of attached (involved with, interested).

impassive As a prefix, *im-* can mean *not*. Let *pass* remind you of *passion*. Putting this prefix and root together, you'll see how **impassive** means, more or less, "not having passion or interest" in something.

listless For this word, simply think *lifeless*.

remote We all know what a **remote** control is! It allows our television to be operated in a **remote** (*distant*) manner. Link this word to that which you already know.

MATCHING

Match the vocabulary words in Column A with *one or more* of their defining characteristics appearing in Column B.

Column A	Column B
1. remote	a. showing no interest
2. apathetic	b. distant
3. detached	c. lacking feeling about something
4. aloof	d. casually unconcerned
5. nonchalant	e. unconcerned

SENTENCE COMPLETION

Remember: Answer choices can be the lesson words themselves, or words that appear in definitions or Memory Tips. Select a word form and part of speech that fit correctly within the sentence.

1. A (an) _____ Saturday afternoon involves the same old errands, the same old lunch haunt, and the same old household chores.
(listless, indifferent, detached, nonchalance, aloof)

2. "I'm happy with either warm destination. It makes no difference to me whether we vacation in Acapulco or in Cabo San Lucas this year," mother remarked in a cheerful, yet _____ tone.
(stolid, nonchalantly, indifferent, remote, stoical)

3. Natalia is more than _____; she is categorically _____, for even if she lost her scholarship, broke up with her boyfriend, and was kicked off the varsity lacrosse team, she would still carry on as if the world revolved smoothly around her.
(detached...listless, nonchalant...stolid, phlegmatic...indifference, detachment....aloofness, apathetic...nonchalance)

4. Even though the snowy, icy cold day made me feel _____ while closed up indoors all day, I still managed to peel, chop, and dice as I cooked up a health brew: hearty chicken soup simmered with seven vegetables.
(stoical, remote, impassively, aloof, phlegmatic)

5. The fact that you have several winter coats to choose from gives you no right to be aloof and _____ regarding children who do not own warm and properly fitting winter clothing.
(stolidly, indifference, impassively, listless, apathetic)

WORDS IN CONTEXT

Based on the context in which each **bold** word is used, identify the word usage of each sentence as either C (Correct) or I (Incorrect).

1. **Impassively**, the science teacher ranted and raved when he learned that the field trip fund was cut by 35 percent.

2. The families were **indifferent** to their weekend vacation; they would have been happy with either going skiing or going outlet shopping.

3. **Nonchalance** about the suffering of humanity is commendable.

4. The annual gathering of his college fraternity was of little interest to Sam; he remained **detached** from the brotherhood.

5. Family values are extremely important. How could one be **aloof** when discussing this topic?

Lesson 14

NO GET UP OR GO!
Words Relating to Lacking Energy or Movement

enervated indolent languor lassitude lethargic sedentary sluggish soporific stagnant static torpid

---

enervated (EN-uhr-vay-tud) *adj*. tired, lacking energy; spent of energy, dissipated

> Gerri's early bird routine finally caught up with her; by Thursday morning she would feel completely **enervated**.

> **Enervated** from an abundance of household chores, Mother collapsed on the couch.

> To a reasonable extent, energized and **enervated** are antonyms.

indolent (IN-duh-lunt) *adj*. lazy; not wanting to do any work

> "The Lazy Boy" is a perfect title for a story about an **indolent** youth.

> **Indolence** kept Alicia from finishing the assignment. I hope she won't be so lazy in the future.

> Kevin deserves his reputation for **indolence**. He spends more time taking breaks than doing the work.

languor (LANG-gur) *n*. a weak or lifeless feeling

> By nine o'clock in the evening, I feel too **languorous** to do anything except watch TV.

> To prevent **languor** in the workplace, the employees do calisthenics for five minutes every two hours.

> The story is about a slow journey down a river flowing **languorously** to the sea.

lassitude (LA-suh-tood) *n.* a tired feeling, usually resulting from depression or too much work

Overcome by **lassitude**, I sat on the porch all day and watched the grass grow.

Lassitude takes hold of him whenever his dad starts telling the same boring stories about the good old days.

Myra felt overwhelming **lassitude** on the hot and humid afternoon. She couldn't even make it to the kitchen for a dish of ice cream.

lethargic (luh-THAR-jik) *adj.* having little or no energy

It takes Herbie two hours to shake off the lifeless feeling of a **lethargic** Monday morning.

Sunday mornings make Otto feel **lethargic**. He rarely stirs from his bed until after noon.

With the **lethargy** lifted, he turns into a human dynamo.

sedentary (SEH-dn-ter-ee) *adj.* having to do with sitting around a lot

Polly has a **sedentary** desk job; she sits all day in front of a computer screen.

A **sedentary** lifestyle caused Paul to become fat and flabby. He vows to start exercising soon.

Keith needs to keep moving. A **sedentary** day leaves him feeling like a marshmallow.

sluggish (SLUH-gish) *adj.* slow and lazy

The drain in the bathtub is **sluggish**. It takes 10 minutes for the water to empty.

According to Coach Meers, a candy bar will keep you from being **sluggish** during practice.

Sluggishness must run in the family. His brother moves like a snail, too.

soporific (sah-puh-RI-fik) *adj.* sleep-inducing; sleepy

A sweet, sugary dessert is as **soporific** as a sleeping pill for Dad. Ten minutes after dinner, he's out like a light.

Driving on a flat interstate highway for a long time is **soporific**. I, for one, have a hard time staying awake.

Coffee is a good anti-**soporific**. At least, it keeps me awake.

stagnant (STAG-nunt) *adj.* lacking movement or energy

A **stagnant** career is one that is not going anywhere.

"Books will keep your mind from **stagnating**," said the teacher.

The still surfaces of **stagnant** pools and ponds encourage the growth of algae.

static (STA-tik) *adj.* lack of movement, change, or development; motionless, stagnant; fixed, immobile

The tech business earnings were **static**, as the gross profits remained stable from the past year to the current year.

Despite his cheerleader girlfriend begging him to take a power walk with her, Mohammed remained **static**, sitting in his chair and watching the ballgame.

Those who live a **static** lifestyle aspire neither to change nor to evolve whether spiritually, socially, or materially.

torpid (TOR-pud) *adj.* lacking energy; relating to inactivity; feeling sluggish

It was hot and muggy—a **torpid**, sleep-inducing day.

Harold felt too **torpid** to do anything but sit on the beach and count the waves.

Lying in the sun, a sweet **torpidity** overcame me, and I soon fell asleep.

MEMORY TIPS

Use these mnemonics (memory devices) to boost your vocabulary. Make up your own memory clues for words in this lesson that are personally challenging. Add these tips—and your own—to your Vocabulary Notebook. Remember, vocabulary building is key to increasing your score on the verbal SAT.

<u>**in**d**ol**en</u>**ce** Simply link this word to *idleness* (laziness). After all, both words have three syllables and sound similar. Notice that *idle* can be spelled from the letters contained in <u>**in**d**ol**en</u>**ce**. Write InDoLEnce in your Vocabulary Notebook.

<u>**languor**</u> Since **languor** is a weak, tired feeling, people who feel languor tend to just hang around or *linger* a lot. Say this chant three times in a row to fix in your mind the meaning of this word: "In **languor**, I linger. In **languor**, I linger. In **languor**, I linger."

<u>**slug**gish</u> Think: Moving "like a <u>slug</u>!" We've all seen slugs gliding along on our patios and walkways. They are s—l—o—w-moving."

<u>**sta**gnant</u> Let the *sta* at the beginning of this word make you think of *staying*, like staying in one place because there's no motion or because there's no energy to move around.

<u>**torpid**</u> The chant "**Torpid** tortoise, **torpid** tortoise, **torpid** tortoise" can help you remember that torpid means sluggish and slow moving.

MATCHING

Match the vocabulary words in Column A with *one or more* of their defining characteristics appearing in Column B.

Column A	Column B
1. sedentary	a. slow-moving
2. soporific	b. feeling tired
3. sluggish	c. sitting around a lot
4. languid	d. sleep-inducing
5. indolent	e. lazy

SENTENCE COMPLETION

Remember: Answer choices can be the lesson words themselves, or words that appear in definitions or Memory Tips. Select a word form and part of speech that fit correctly within the sentence.

1. A (an) _____ lifestyle is one that is going nowhere fast: no new employment, no new love interest, no volunteer work, and no new life-changing commitments.
   (soporific, lethargic, lassitude, indolent, stagnant)

2. Even though Justin was simply feeling _____, those who observed him interpreted his languor as an indication of his unrespectable _____.
   (languid...sedentary, torpid...indolence, stagnating...lethargy, lethargic...torpidity, indolent...lassitude)

3. Nomadic hunters and gatherers, wandering Indian tribes, and early American settlers—the last thing one can call these industrious groups of people is _____.
   (soporific, lethargy, sedentary, sluggishly, languor)

4. Filled with a heavy feeling of _____, all I could manage to do all day was read a little, then rest on the couch, then read a little more, then watch television on the couch.
   (stagnant, soporific, torpid, sluggish, languor)

5. Chamomile tea with a drizzle of honey and a trickle of lemon makes a _____ potion that suddenly puts me into a warm, soothing sleep.
   (soporific, languid, torpid, listless, stagnant)

WORDS IN CONTEXT

Based on the context in which each **bold** word is used, identify the word usage of each sentence as either C (Correct) or I (Incorrect).

1. **Languid** people are likely to simply hang around.

2. **Soporific** vitamins boost athletic performance.

3. A bad attitude is necessarily a sign of **sluggishness**.

4. Ms. Green's bad knee makes her lifestyle increasingly **sedentary**.

5. **Indolence** is bliss for someone who dislikes work.

Lesson 15

IS THERE ANYTHING I CAN DO FOR YOU, MASTER?

Words Relating to Humility and Obedience

---

compliant fawning obsequious oppressed servile slavish subjugated submissive subordinate subservient sycophant toady

---

compliant (kum-PLY-unt) *adj.* yielding, submissive

Ms. Hayes prefers **compliant** students, those who'll do everything they are told.

If you **comply** with the school rules, you won't get into trouble.

Rose always **complies** with Charles' requests. She never says no.

fawning (FAW-ning) *adj.* gaining the favor of another by acting overly kind or by using flattery

Mike advised me to stop **fawning** over Dawn. "She'll like you just as well even if you don't overindulge her," he said.

Fawning is a form of manipulation to win favors and get what you want from others.

As a **fawning** advisor to the Queen, Peters told Her Majesty only what she wanted to hear.

obsequious (ub-SEE-kwee-us) *adj.* obeying or performing a service for someone in an overly attentive manner

Uriah practiced **obsequiousness** by always telling others what a privilege it was to be of service to them.

Some teachers prefer **obsequious** students who fawn over them.

Hoping for a big tip, the waiter oozed **obsequiousness**, constantly flattering me and calling me "sir."

oppressed (uh-PREST) *adj.* harshly dominated; troubled and stressed; dominated in a cruel and inhumane manner

The greedy government **oppressed** its citizens with a heavy tax burden and insurmountable civic duties.

Feeling **oppressed** by a demanding seventy-hour work week and a long commute, the business executive reinvented himself and became the principal of a thriving business that suited his interests.

Oppressed and browbeaten, the underpaid workers went on strike, demanding a pay raise as well as improvement in working conditions and benefits.

servile (SUR-vul) *adj.* slave-like; very humble and submissive

Roy has no right to treat you like a **servile** lackey. You are not his slave or valet.

I hate having a **servile** job. It's not in my nature to bow to the whims of others.

Susan's **servility** caused her to cater to everyone's desires but her own.

slavish (SLAY-vish) *adj.* slave-like; overly humble; involving very hard work

Nicole worked **slavishly** in the kitchen preparing dinner for 30 guests.

Harry followed Sally around, **slavishly** attending to her every need.

Don had a **slavish** sidekick who did the dirty work and devoted himself to Don's well-being.

subjugated (SUB-jih-gay-tid) *adj.* brought under another's or another entity's complete control; mastered; conquered; made subservient, submissive; enslaved

Gia's intimidation tactics **subjugated** him into a state of mental anguish, fear, and immobility.

Within weeks of taking office, the new mayor **subjugated** the tax payers to his grand infrastructure rebuild.

The aliens **subjugated** the Earthlings soon after their colossal flying saucer landed.

submissive (sub-MIH-siv) *adj.* voluntarily obeying another; humble

Lauren was attracted to **submissive** friends, people who'd do everything she asked of them.

Over time, Lenny learned to be less **submissive**. He actually stood up to George once in a while.

A recruit has to be **submissive** to the sergeant or he's going to get into big trouble.

subordinate (suh-BOR-duh-nit) *adj.* inferior; lower in rank or status

In a sentence, a **subordinate** (dependent) clause depends on the main (independent) clause for its meaning.

The sailor was accused of **insubordination** after defying the lieutenant's order.

For the sake of good discipline, officers are forbidden to fraternize with their **subordinate** unit members.

subservient (sub-SUR-vee-unt) *adj.* obedient; obsequious

In my grandmother's day, a wife was expected to be **subservient** to her husband.

Ricky asked **subserviently**, "May I please be excused, sir, for just a minute or two?"

The apprentice played a **subservient** role, trying to serve his master in every way.

sycophant (SIH-kuh-funt) *n.* a self-server who tries to gain the favor of others through the use of flattery or by being overattentive

The king couldn't distinguish the honest advisers from the **sycophants** who flattered him for personal gain.

Myron couldn't get a promotion on his merits, so he got one by being a **sycophant** to his boss.

Jason made a **sycophantic** speech full of praise and flattery for the chairman.

toady (TOE-dee) *n.* a flatterer; a sycophant

Hoping to win the coach's favor, James became the coach's **toady**.

If Mary were less of a **toady**, she wouldn't follow the teacher around so much.

Volunteering to wash the coach's car shows what a **toady** Karen has become.

MEMORY TIPS

Use these mnemonics (memory devices) to boost your vocabulary. Make up your own memory clues for words in this lesson that are personally challenging. Add these tips—and your own—to your Vocabulary Notebook.

fawning To help you remember the meaning of this word, picture a fawn, which is a young deer. Since a fawn is gentle and young he is more likely to *cringe* in the presence of bigger, stronger animals and *cater* to them.

servile, slavish These vocabulary words *contain* the keys to their definitions! Servile, servant-like. Slavish, slave-like.

subjugated, submissive, subordinate, subservient The prefix *sub-*, meaning *below* or *under*, is key to these vocabulary words. Think of additional words you know, like submarine, subhuman, substitute, and subzero.

MATCHING

Match the vocabulary words in Column A with *one or more* of their defining characteristics appearing in Column B.

Column A	Column B
1. toady	a. slave-like
2. sycophant	b. a brown-noser
3. subservient	c. lower in rank
4. subordinate	d. flatterer
5. slavish	e. obedient

SENTENCE COMPLETION

Remember: Answer choices can be the lesson words themselves, or words that appear in definitions or Memory Tips. Select a word form and part of speech that fit correctly within the sentence.

1. Tod is nobody's _____; if someone asks him to jump, he doesn't respond, "How high?" Instead, Tod says, "No, *you* jump!" (fawning, subservience, slavish, obsequious, toady)

2. Chuck is more than _____ —he is downright _____ and will dutifully perform almost any task you ask of him to your exact specifications and requirements. (subordinate...submissive, compliant...subservient, slavish...fawning, sycophantic...submission, slavishness...yielding)

3. Although Hank appears outgoing and bold on camera, in person he is a living picture of docility and _____. (toady, sycophantic, subordinate, submissiveness, servile)

4. Stop _____ over Julianna; for once, let her make her own breakfast and prepare her own cup of morning latté! (subservience, slavishness, insubordination, servility, fawning)

5. For some women, homemaking is _____ to having a career; for others, raising a family and taking care of their homes is the most gratifying of life's callings. (toady, slavish, subordinate, subservient, fawning)

WORDS IN CONTEXT

Based on the context in which each **bold** word is used, identify the word usage of each sentence as either C (Correct) or I (Incorrect).

1. My **subservient** roommate always demands her way.

2. **Fawning** over another makes the object of your attention feel worthless.

3. Always busy, a **toady** is likely to get burned out.

4. In the classroom, a **sycophant** might be called a "brown-noser."

5. It's surprising to witness how Harold, towering a foot and a half over his wife, acts so **submissively** toward his mate.

Review Exercises / Lessons 11–15

VOCABULARY-IN-CONTEXT PARAGRAPH

The paragraph below primarily features words that appear in vocabulary lessons 11–15. For added reinforcement, additional vocabulary words from other lessons may appear in the paragraph. In those cases, the lesson number in which those words appear is indicated within parentheses. In light of the context, the words' meanings should be clear. If you are uncertain about particular meanings, however, take a moment to review the word's definition and illustrative sentences, as provided within the referenced lessons.

Lessons 11–15: Student-Athlete

In the life of a student-athlete, there is no room for *lassitude*. A *sluggish* body or mind is *deleterious* to one's performance in the classroom, as well as on the football field. If a student is *impassive* or borderline *indifferent* about swimming, soccer, or lacrosse, he should not commit to the school team. He will ultimately be *derided* by his coach, teammates, and game spectators for his *indolence*. Even when facing essay deadlines, quarterly exams, and long-term projects, student-athletes must be *subservient* to their coaches' rigorous schedule of three-hour-long practices and *comply* with early morning scrimmages and playoff games on the weekends. In fact, a *nonchalant* attitude may lead to various forms of *censure*.

NAME THAT CLUSTER

To the left of the groups of words, put the Roman numeral that corresponds with these theme (or cluster) titles:

Words Relating to . . .

I. Lacking Energy or Movement
II. Harmful or Mean
III. Humility and Obedience
IV. Lacking Interest or Emotion
V. Criticizing, Disapproving, or Scolding

Cluster Title _____   1. virulent, deleterious, pernicious, baneful, nefarious

Cluster Title _____   2. lethargic, sedentary, lassitude, indolent, torpid

Cluster Title _____   3. censure, castigate, disparage, condemn, rebuke

Cluster Title _____   4. submissive, toady, fawning, slavish, compliant

Cluster Title _____   5. nonchalant, remote, phlegmatic, stolid, impassive

---

SENTENCE COMPLETION

Note: On the new SAT (March 2016 and forward), multiple-choice sentence completion questions have been eliminated. However, sentence completion questions remain in this book as a vocabulary-strengthening exercise. Make flashcards for the words that are unknown or unfamiliar to you.

Read the sentence through carefully. Then, from the five vocabulary words given in parentheses, circle the word that fits *best*.

1. Mr. McKee spent five hours every night in his recliner, watching television. His evenings were _____.
   (malicious, compliant, sedentary, stolid, aloof)

2. After eating too many sweets, Kipper felt _____. He just didn't feel like getting off the couch for *anything*.
   (sluggish, remote, ominous, subordinate, fawning)

3. The youngest child, Anna, jumped at her three older brothers' commands. She played a _____ role in the family.
   (phlegmatic, baneful, odious, submissive, listless)

4. "Stop _____ all over your father!" yelled Mom. "*He* can get up and get himself a Diet Coke for once!"
   (detrimental, languid, fawning, toady, stagnating)

5. "Coating people's cars with raw egg and smashing pumpkins on front stoops is _____ even when it's Halloween," our neighbor stated firmly.
(torpid, compliant, indifferent, obsequious, nefarious)

6. A (An) _____ youth, Tyler lounges around all day long in his typical, _____ manner.
indolent...sycophantic
effervescent...panegyric
submissive...baneful
sluggish...nefarious
lethargic...sedentary

7. Although Patty comes across as _____ when it comes to nature and the outdoors, she is actually a (an) _____ gardener.
deleterious...submissive
compliant...zealous
stolid...listless
apathetic...avid
castigating...odious

8. Unless you want to be called a "doormat," stop being so _____ all the time!
(virulent, compliant, listless, chastised, soporific)

9. To avoid the _____ consequences of pesticides, Rachel purchased only organic produce from local farm markets.
(devious, fawning, indifferent, deleterious, stagnant)

10. With exciting activities planned for the week—such as cruising in a glass-bottom boat, riding wave runners, and watching kite surfers—the boys did not have a single moment of _____ or _____ while vacationing in picturesque Cabo San Lucas.
fawning...iniquity
carping...compliance
listlessness...lethargy
subservience...castigation
detriment...nonchalance

ONE DOESN'T BELONG

Three of the words in each grouping relate to each other somehow. Cross off the one word that does not belong with the others. For a challenge, write the word that does not belong on the line below, and try your best to define that word. *Note:* Some of the words have been taken from definitions or exercises that appear within the lessons.

1. deprecate   impugn   rebuff   iniquitous

   _____ means _____

2. stolid   subordinate   indifferent   detached

   _____ means _____

3. toady   sycophant   impassive   fawning

   _____ means _____

4. loathsome   odious   nefarious   obsequious

   _____ means _____

5. aloof   berate   disinterested   listless

   _____ means _____

ardent avid ebullient effervescent exuberant fanatical fervent impassioned vibrant zealous

---

ardent (AR-dnt) *adj.* full of passion and emotion

Ardent soccer fans never miss a game.

John and Sherrie's embrace was more than a casual hug; it was an **ardent** show of affection.

For their extraordinary service, the volunteers deserve **ardent** thanks.

avid (A-vud) *adj.* showing enthusiasm; ardent

Walt is an **avid** hiker; he never misses a chance to hit the trail.

An **avid** skier, Sue will drive for hours to be where the snow is.

For years my dad has been an **avid** golfer, out on the links every weekend.

ebullient (ih-BOOL-yunt) *adj.* filled with a bubbly excitement, as if boiling over with excitement

The audience became just as enthusiastic about following the diet as the **ebullient** speaker was in describing it.

His **ebullience** was infectious. Everyone left the room filled with excitement about the rafting trip.

Having made a hole in one, Tiger could hardly contain his **ebullience**.

effervescent (eh-fur-VEH-snt) *adj.* lively; full of uplifted spirit; vivacious

Distressed over losing the car keys, Beth was less **effervescent** than usual.

The root beer had lost its **effervescence** and tasted like bad cough syrup.

Laura is quiet and subdued, but her twin Lara epitomizes **effervescence**.

exuberant (ig-ZOO-buh-runt) *adj.* overflowing with vitality and good spirits

As a night owl, Amelia feels most **exuberant** between ten o'clock and midnight.

Worry and anxiety can put a damper on even the most **exuberant** personality.

The next morning he leaped from bed **exuberantly**, anticipating the adventures of the day.

[fan]atical (fuh-NA-tih-kul) *adj.* full of great enthusiasm or devotion

Clark is a **fanatical** bowler. His head is filled with thoughts of strikes and spares, balls and alleys.

Louise's mom is **fanatical** about cleaning the house. She won't let you in unless you take your shoes off.

I don't eat red meat, but I'm not **fanatical** about it.

[f]ervent (FUR-vunt) *adj.* filled with passion or intensity

The minister asked her congregation to pray **fervently** for the safe return of the lost child.

He's a **fervent** cat breeder. Nothing is as important to him as raising cats.

She's a nut for crossword puzzles, but she hasn't always been so **fervent** about doing them.

impassioned (im-PA-shund) *adj.* filled with passionate emotion

The defense attorney made an **impassioned** speech to the jury, but the jury remained unmoved by his emotional words.

Because Tino's **impassioned** words struck Maria's heart, she agreed to marry him.

King Henry's **impassioned** speech to his troops raised their morale and contributed to their victory in battle.

vibrant (VIE-brunt) *adj.* lively; full of vitality

> Marilyn and Curt are an unlikely couple. She's so **vibrant**, and he's as quiet as a corpse.

> Although the bright hues clash sometimes, all of Diana's clothes have **vibrant** colors.

> His **vibrant** teaching keeps the class lively.

zealous (ZEH-lus) *adj.* filled with enthusiasm; fervent

> A **zealous** bodybuilder, Derek works out in the weight room during every spare moment.

> If everyone were as **zealous** a worker as Scott, there would be no need for a supervisor.

> Jorge is a **zealous** reader of mysteries. As soon as he finishes one book, he starts reading the next.

MEMORY TIPS

Use these mnemonics (memory devices) to boost your vocabulary. Make up your own memory clues for words in this lesson that are personally challenging. Add these tips—and your own—to your Vocabulary Notebook. Remember, vocabulary building is key to increasing your score on the verbal SAT.

ebullient Let *bull* remind you of strong. Next, let the initial e stand for enthusiasm or excitement. "Strong enthusiasm/excitement" is a concise working definition for this vocabulary word.

fanatical Is this a new vocabulary word for you? I bet it's not. You already know what a *fan* is, right? Think of sports fan, Britney Spears fan, NSync fan, and so on. Simply link your understanding of *fan* to the meaning of **fanatical** (acting like a *fan*.)

fervent Scramble the first five letters to get *fever*. Next, connect *fever* (something hot, burning) to "full of passion," which is the kernel definition of **fervent**. Write **fervent** in red ink in your Vocabulary Notebook. Use red for passion.

MATCHING

Match the vocabulary words in Column A with *one or more* of their defining characteristics appearing in Column B.

Column A	Column B
1. ebullient	a. filled with passion
2. ardent	b. overly devoted
3. impassioned	c. bubbling with enthusiasm
4. effervescent	d. avid
5. fanatical	e. full of lively spirit

SENTENCE COMPLETION

Remember: *Answer choices can be the lesson words themselves, or words that appear in definitions or Memory Tips. Select a word form and part of speech that fit correctly within the sentence.*

1. Daily commitment shows that, above all else, Melanie is very _____ about her exercise routine and her macrobiotic diet.
   (fervent, ebullient, vivacious, vibrant, exuberantly)

2. Brian's is an all-around buoyant spirit; whether washing his car, shopping for toiletries, or doing the bills, he wears a broad smile that reflects his inner _____.
   (ebullience, fanaticism, zeal, avidness, vibrant)

3. Thirty minutes of exercise three times a week is beneficial, but thirty minutes of exercise three times a day is downright _____!
   (ardent, avid, effervescent, impassioned, fanatical)

4. _____ when it comes to flavoring his culinary concoctions in abundance, Mario buys nearly every seasoning blend, spice, and fresh herb he can get his hands on.
   (Zealous, Vibrant, Fanaticism, Ebullience, Fervently)

5. With a wide smile, lively eyes, and a _____ voice, Janice is a welcome addition to every social gathering because she imparts a festive and vivacious spirit.
   (vitality, fanatical, vibrant, zeal, ebullience)

WORDS IN CONTEXT

Based on the context in which each **bold** word is used, identify the word usage of each sentence as either C (Correct) or I (Incorrect).

1. Ana's **impassioned** letter lacks strong emotion.

2. The **fervent** sports manager neglected his leadership responsibilities.

3. Envy is a likely character flaw of a **zealous** individual.

4. A **fervent** NSync follower, Gus never missed one of their concerts or MTV specials.

5. John, an **ardent** fast food entrepreneur, steadfastly pursued his aims and goals despite many setbacks.

LIKE A MULE
Words Relating to Being Stubborn

adamant dogmatic hidebound intractable obdurate
obstinate recalcitrant resolve unwavering unyielding willful

adamant (A-duh-munt) *adj.* unwilling to bend; unyielding

Although the invitation said dress was formal, Chucky was **adamant** about wearing track shoes to the prom.

Dad's **adamant** tone convinced him there was no chance he could go dressed like that.

Mom **adamantly** refused my request for Coca-Cola at breakfast.

dogmatic (dog-MA-tik) *adj.* strongly opinionated; rigid; dictatorial

Dogmatic Doug was so set in his convictions that he would not even listen to viewpoints that were expressed by another person.

Dogmatic religious beliefs are rooted in firm principles and rigid codes of conduct.

Pleading for permission to sleep at her friend's house, Beth sulked when her mother answered with a **dogmatic** "No!" This topic was not open for discussion.

hidebound (HIDE-bound) *adj.* strongly opinionated; narrow-mindedly stubborn

Dad is a **hidebound** Boston fan; he has rooted for the Red Sox all his life.

A **hidebound** vegetarian, Vera turned down a free hot dog at the ball game.

Hidebound and set in his ways, Grandpa will not eat anything for dinner unless it's meat and potatoes.

intractable (in-TRAK-tuh-bul) *adj.* stubborn; hard to manage

Because neither his teachers nor his counselor could control Ivan's **intractable** behavior, he was sent to the psychologist for testing.

An **intractable** nature cannot easily be tamed.

Rose forced open the **intractable** window with a screwdriver.

obdurate (AHB-duh-rut) *adj.* resistant to persuasion or softening; stubbornly persistent in wrongdoing

The killer showed no remorse for his deed. For being **obdurate**, he was sentenced to life in prison.

Steve stuck to his opinion **obdurately** in spite of evidence that proved him wrong.

Senator McCain was unwilling to compromise. By being **obdurate**, he finally got the bill passed.

obstinate (AHB-stuh-nut) *adj.* stubborn; inflexible

Despite an allergy to chocolate, Charlotte **obstinately** refused to give up her daily bag of M&M's.

"Don't be so **obstinate**," pleaded Mother. "Try having an open mind instead."

The teacher **obstinately** refused to believe that Harold wrote the paper himself.

recalcitrant (rih-KAL-suh-trunt) *adj.* stubborn, disobedient; defiant

The **recalcitrant** boy in the back row refused to turn off his cell phone during class.

In spite of the law, many **recalcitrant** drivers resist putting on seat belts.

The usher asked the moviegoers to form an orderly line, but the **recalcitrant** crowd wouldn't budge.

Lesson 18

SOUND SENSATIONS

Words Relating to Sound

acoustics cacophony clamor din discordant euphony
mellifluous raucous strident vociferous

---

acoustics (uh-KOOS-tiks) *n.* the quality of sound, pertaining to how it is heard based on the quality and structure of the room

At first the sound inside Philharmonic Hall was flat, but after the renovation the **acoustics** were perfect.

The sound track of the film was extraordinary. Whoever handled the sound must have been an **acoustic** genius.

Always fascinated by sound, Ernest studied to be an **acoustical** engineer.

cacophony (ka-KAH-fuh-nee) *n.* lack of harmony; loud and unpleasant noise; a racket

The clash of metal on the rocks created a **cacophony** that was hard to bear.

The mix of harsh sounds in the streets of the city creates a **cacophony**.

Unlike old-fashioned melodic music, ultra-modern music often consists of lots of **cacophonous** sounds.

clamor (KLA-mur) *n.* unpleasant sound; noise

The **clamor** of a crowing rooster and clucking hens woke up the farmer.

How can I concentrate with that **clamor** of pots and dishes going on in the kitchen?

Earphones muffled the **clamor**, allowing Davy to listen to the music in peace.

resolve (rih-ZAHLV) *n.* firmness, determination

"Don't doubt my **resolve**," said Holly. "I will definitely become a famous fashion designer one day."

"Rely on your inner **resolve** to just say 'no' to drugs," said nurse Betty.

After a disastrous first grading period, Shawn **resolved** to do better during the next one.

unwavering (un-WAVE-ring) *adj.* firm and determined

Trudy's **unwavering** desire to lose weight kept her on the all-pineapple diet for a month.

Hoping for an 800 on the verbal section of the SAT, Dave **unwaveringly** studied every vocabulary word in the book.

Instead of abandoning the president in time of trouble, many people stood by him **unwaveringly**.

unyielding (un-YEEL-ding) *adj.* stubborn; inflexible

Whenever Cecile asked her father to buy her a car, her dad gave her the same **unyielding** answer: "Not a chance!"

Ms. Grace practices **unyielding** courtesy. She never fails to thank a student for handing in a homework assignment.

The troops fought with an **unyielding** ferocity, never stopping until they had won the battle.

willful (WIL-ful) *adj.* stubborn

It makes no sense to **willfully** ignore the evidence against smoking.

Jill knows that she's a **willful** brat who insists on always getting her way.

Vandalizing the poster was no accident. It was done **willfully**.

MEMORY TIPS

Use these mnemonics (memory devices) to boost your vocabulary. Make up your own memory clues for words in this lesson that are personally challenging. Add these tips—and your own—to your Vocabulary Notebook.

dogmatic The stem for this word is *dogma*. A dogma is a rigid set of beliefs or principles, or a set of beliefs held as unquestionable truth. Therefore, a person who is **dogmatic** has his or her beliefs and ideas rooted in dogma.

hidebound Did you know that "hide" is another word for leather (buckskin, pigskin, etc.)? Imagine a person wrapped tight in "hide," so set in her opinion that she won't budge. Picture it? In other words, a **hidebound** individual is unwavering, unyielding, unwilling to "give a little." Someone **hidebound** is stubborn, set in his or her ways.

obdurate, obstinate Learn these two words meaning *stubborn* as a pair. After all, they both start off with *ob*, and they both have three syllables. In addition, if you study or speak Italian, you may know that "dura" means hard. So **obdurate** means *hard-headed*, which is slang for *stubborn*. Whether you know some Italian or not, it's smart to always consider the vocabulary you know from your second or third language. Memory clues that are formed from foreign language connections are very effective and fun.

SENTENCE COMPLETION

Remember: *Answer choices can be the lesson words themselves, or words that appear in definitions or Memory Tips. Select a word form and part of speech that fit correctly within the sentence.*

1. Unlike a spineless jelly fish, a (an) _____ individual wears a tough hide and has a sturdy backbone.
   (obdurately, obstinate, resolve, defiance, willfulness)

2. _____ to a fault when his mind is made up, Jake has the backbone of a horse and the determination of a jet plane on a mission.
   (Adamantly, Recalcitrance, Wavering, Resolve, Unyielding)

3. Although Julie has urged Jack many times to use his cellular phone in the car only with his hands-free speaker device, _____ Jack continues to gab on his cell, leaving just one hand on the steering wheel.
   (yielding, resolve, recalcitrant, obduracy, tractable)

4. The Labradoodle puppy was much more than a challenge to manage— she was _____. Two-year-old Baci, however, who lounges around and sleeps most of the day, is ten times more docile and submissive.
   (dogmatic, intractable, adamantly, hidebound, resolved)

5. You're so _____ that your head must be made of cement and your mind must wear a sign that reads, "Closed to Outside Ideas."
   (willfully, yielding, intractable, obdurate, dogma)

WORDS IN CONTEXT

Based on the context in which each **bold** word is used, identify the word usage of each sentence as either C (Correct) or I (Incorrect).

1. Once Brandon has his mind set, there's no changing it; he's an **unwavering** young man.

2. **Intractable** individuals are the easiest to control.

3. When it comes to homework, Mother is **adamant** about it getting done sometime after school or, perhaps, soon after dinner. Otherwise, Mom wants it finished by 11 P.M.

4. An **obstinate** child is easily led by his peers.

5. **Resolved** to get her first children's book published, Lillian set aside a minimum of five hours a day for writing and marketing.

din (DIN) *n.* ongoing loud sound; noise

When Bernie hit the grand slam, the **din** in Yankee Stadium could be heard all the way to City Hall.

The farmyard **din** astonished Farmer Jones. He had never heard all his animals bellowing so loudly.

The **din** of the bulldozer at work next door made it impossible for us to hear each other.

discordant (dis-KOR-dnt) *adj.* lacking harmony or agreement

Instead of beautiful melodies, Berg wrote **discordant** notes that grate on the ear.

All agreed to the decision until Paul brought up the **discordant** fact that our group lacked the authority to make such decisions.

The first sign of **discord** between Jenny and Harvey was the shouting match they had one day after school.

euphony (YOO-fuh-nee) *n.* pleasing sound

While I rested in bed under a cozy blanket, the **euphony** of raindrops on the roof soon lulled me to sleep.

Junior's violin screeching sounded **euphonious** only to his parents. Everyone else covered their ears.

The sound of a school bell, while irritating to others, is **euphony** to me.

mellifluous (meh-LIH-fluh-wus) *adj.* sweet and smooth sounding

Mother's **mellifluous** singing voice was so sweet and soothing that the baby fell asleep in seconds.

Because of his **mellifluous** voice, Grant was hired as a radio announcer.

The **mellifluous** tones of an Irish tenor floated through my hotel window in Dublin.

raucous (RAW-kus) *adj.* coarse-sounding; loud and unruly

The **raucous** band prevented us from hearing each other speak, so we used gestures and pantomime.

As the princess's motorcade came closer, the crowd grew **raucous**, and when she arrived, the din was impossible.

The **raucous** strikers yelled obscenities at passersby.

strident (STRY-dnt) *adj.* shrill; high-pitched

> Joe started off with some harsh words that set a **strident** tone for the whole meeting.

> It's hard to take the **strident** sound of the school bell so early in the morning.

> The geese flew south, leaving the **strident** sound of their honks behind them.

vociferous (voh-SIH-frus) *adj.* loud and noisy regarding one's own voice, especially shouting; demandingly clamorous

> Danny **vociferously** denied cutting class. He wouldn't stop shouting about it for hours.

> The **vociferous** crowd noisily demanded that the store open its doors. "Open up or else," they shouted.

> I couldn't help overhearing the **vociferous** altercation that took place in the waiting room. It was too loud to ignore.

MEMORY TIPS

Use these mnemonics (memory devices) to boost your vocabulary. Make up your own memory clues for words in this lesson that are personally challenging. Add these tips—and your own—to your Vocabulary Notebook.

cacophony, euphony These words both contain *phon*, which is the root having to do with sound. Knowledge of this root alone is very helpful in recognizing the meanings of these words. Prefixes are helpful to know, too. *Eu-* indicates *good*, as in euphoria and euphemism, for example. (Look these up!) *Caco-*, a derivative of the Greek "kakos," indicates *bad*. Did you know that cacography means bad handwriting and/or poor spelling?

mellifluous Repeat this chant aloud three times in a row: "**Mellifluous** melodies, **mellifluous** melodies, **mellifluous** melodies." This alliterative chant should remind you that melodies are sweet-sounding, smooth-sounding; in other words, **mellifluous**. Write this chant three times in your Vocabulary Notebook.

vociferous The Latin root *voc* refers to *voice*. Other words containing this root include vocal, vocalize, and vocalist.

MATCHING

Match the vocabulary words in Column A with *one or more* of their defining characteristics appearing in Column B.

Column A	Column B
1. euphony	a. relating to the science of sound
2. din	b. harsh-sounding
3. cacophonous	c. having to do with loud voices
4. acoustics	d. consistent, loud noise
5. vociferous	e. pleasing sound
6. mellifluous	f. smooth-sounding

SENTENCE COMPLETION

Remember: Answer choices can be the lesson words themselves, or words that appear in definitions or Memory Tips. Select a word form and part of speech that fit correctly within the sentence.

1. Resonating with some of the best sound quality in the world, the ceiling of Lincoln Center's Avery Fischer Hall is a (an) _____ masterpiece.
   (euphonious, clamorous, strident, vociferous, acoustical)

2. The dog is barking, the television is blaring, and the oven fan is whizzing; please speak louder because I can't hear you above all this _____!
   (din, euphony, mellifluousness, discordant, acoustical)

3. Francis has a _____ voice that earned him high honors in the New York State Music and Arts Festival last summer.
   (discordant, shrill, vociferous, clamorous, mellifluous)

4. Janna is not sure which harsh noise disconcerted her more—the blood-curdling shrieks of the preschool children as they swarmed onto the playground, or the _____ sounds of the school monitors' whistles, blaring and high-pitched.
   (shrill, euphonious, mellifluous, din, acoustical)

5. Whereas the sounds of a baby cooing and crying at two o'clock in the afternoon are pleasant and endearing, those same sounds at two in the morning are unequivocally _____.
(mellifluous, din, euphonious, discordant, discord)

WORDS IN CONTEXT

Based on the context in which each **bold** word is used, identify the word usage of each sentence as either C (Correct) or I (Incorrect).

1. The **acoustics** enjoyed at Avery Fisher Hall are among the best world-wide.

2. Upon entering her friend's home, the woman let out a **strident** "Yooo-Whoooo!" that startled the homeowner.

3. Do you prefer peaceful evenings or **clamorous** mornings?

4. Do you like to **din** more so at friends' houses or at restaurants?

5. The **euphony** of the heavenly violins lingered pleasantly in Mia's memory for hours after the concert's conclusion.

HOW WONDERFUL YOU ARE!

Words Relating to Praise and Respect

acclaim accolade adulate deference esteem eulogize exalt extol laud panegyrize revere venerate

---

acclaim (uh-KLAME) *v.* to express strong approval or praise; hail

He's an accomplished artist, **acclaimed** by all the critics.

Dad was happy to hear his son's talent **acclaimed** by his teachers.

It is a hit play, but in spite of all the **acclaim** it has received, I didn't think much of it.

accolade (A-kuh-lade) *n.* an award given as a sign of appreciation or respect

The Broadway diva received many **accolades** for her stellar performance.

Inclusion in the Zagat's restaurant guide is one of the greatest **accolades** any fine eatery can receive.

For the young soccer player, each trophy that his team received was an **accolade**, commending both their team spirit and dedication.

adulate (A-juh-late) *v.* to praise or flatter too greatly; fawn over

Students who are **adulated** often end up with swelled heads, but not Sean. In spite of the awe he inspires, he's very modest.

Personally, I don't **adulate** him, but I admire and respect his many talents.

Sean received the **adulation** for being both the valedictorian and the school's outstanding athlete.

deference (DEH-fuh-runts) *n.* respect; a level of high esteem or admiration

Married for more than fifty years, Jose spoke with calm **deference** toward his wife, as he asked her opinion of the matter.

In **deference** to her friend's well-kept home, Mrs. Shelton asked her child to remove his sneakers before entering the house.

Exhibiting **deference** toward another is not a sign of weakness but a gesture of magnanimity and strength.

esteem (ih-STEEM) *v.* to value highly; to have great regard for

Bernard is a well-known philanthropist. Far and wide he is highly **esteemed** for his generosity.

Ms. Boyd was **esteemed** by both her employers and her colleagues for all her hard work over the years.

To show how highly they **esteemed** her, they gave her $1 million in stock options when she retired.

eulogize (YOO-luh-jize) *v.* to praise, as in a eulogy; to say good things about

Loretta knew Mike well and **eulogized** the good deeds for which he'll be remembered.

The minister's sermon comforted the grieving family, who appreciated hearing him **eulogize** Grandma's kind and loving spirit.

The introduction sounds like a **eulogy**. While full of praise for the author, it is written in the past tense as though he had already died.

exalt (ig-ZAWLT) *v.* to praise or glorify; to lift up in status, dignity, or power

As the honored leader of the organization, she was **exalted** by the members.

Once **exalted** by the Russian people, Stalin is now a devil in their eyes.

The church plans to **exalt** Mother Teresa by making her a saint.

extol (ik-STOLE) *v.* to praise highly; laud

Extolling the efforts of students never fails to motivate them to keep up the good work.

Those who **extolled** JFK in the past ate their words when some of his less than admirable qualities became public.

The piano teacher **extolled** Johnny's playing, but Johnny's performance revealed that he didn't deserve such high praise.

laud (LAWD) *v.* to praise; extol

He **lauded** my efforts to help, but I didn't think the praise was sincere.

The **laudatory** comments on the back cover suggest that this is a terrific book.

To fly solo across the Atlantic in 1927 was a remarkable achievement, for which Lindbergh was **lauded** by the people everywhere.

panegyrize (PA-nuh-jih-rize) *v.* to praise a person or event in a formal speech or in writing; to praise highly

Mr. Don was asked to say a word in praise of the artist, but he got carried away and **panegyrized** the embarrassed young woman.

As best man at the wedding, Luke **panegyrized** the happy couple.

Before presenting the award, Miss America **panegyrized** this year's winner.

revere (rih-VEER) *v.* to regard highly with love and respect

Ivan's essays were **revered** for their far-reaching wisdom and clarity of thought.

To **revere** the Founding Fathers is part of the formula for making a speech on the Fourth of July.

The Joads **revered** the land, but the landlord didn't care how much they loved it, and chose to evict them.

venerate (VEH-nuh-rate) *v.* to feel or show deep respect for, especially due to age or tradition; to honor

Most religions expect believers to **venerate** old customs and traditions.

The scholar, now old and frail, was still **venerated** by his former colleagues.

Few people still **venerate** lawyers and politicians merely because of the positions they hold.

MEMORY TIPS

Use these mnemonics (memory devices) to boost your vocabulary. Make up your own memory clues for words in this lesson that are challenging for you. Add these tips—and your own—to your Vocabulary Notebook.

laud If you know *applaud*, then simply connect the new word **laud** to the word you already know, *applaud*. The meanings of these two verbs are closely connected. *Plaudits* means praise.

revere You remember Paul Revere from American History, right? Now, I'm sure you'll agree that it's only right to respect, or **revere**, one of our nation's Founding Fathers!

Another tip: You can repeat this chant to yourself over and over "**Revere** the Reverend. **Revere** the Reverend. **Revere** the Reverend."

MATCHING

Match the vocabulary words in Column A with *one or more* of their defining characteristics appearing in Column B.

Column A

1. acclaim
2. adulate
3. revere
4. eulogize
5. exalt
6. panegyrize

Column B

a. to praise in formal writing
b. to praise highly
c. to glorify or lift up in dignity
d. to regard highly with respect
e. to overly praise; fawn over
f. to speak words in praise of someone at a funeral or mass

SENTENCE COMPLETION

Remember: Answer choices can be the lesson words themselves, or words that appear in definitions or Memory Tips. Select a word form and part of speech that fit correctly within the sentence.

1. Interestingly, to word enthusiasts at least, venerate and _____ are synonyms, and the latter can be spelled using the letters found within venerate.
   (extol, laud, panegyrize, eulogize, revere)

2. The student's scientific research on lipid metabolism was so cutting-edge that a national journal _____ the student's work prominently in a special column titled "The Groundbreaking Research of Science Students."
   (lauded, extolling, panegyrized, esteem, adulation)

3. The _____ Judge McKinley, serving his twenty-fifth year in this courthouse, has now entered the courtroom; take your seats and show him the utmost respect throughout this trial.
   (venerable, extolling, laud, accolades, panegyrizing)

4. Some people attend charity events and give big gifts at parties for the _____ they receive publicly; others do good deeds in private, foregoing the public recognition for an inner sense of altruism.
   (laudatory, acclaimed, dignity, adulation, hail)

5. The talented teacher received _____ in abundance for her professional dedication, advisory commitments, and charismatic teaching style.
   (accolades, extol, eulogized, esteemed, laudatory)

WORDS IN CONTEXT

Based on the context in which each **bold** word is used, identify the word usage of each sentence as either C (Correct) or I (Incorrect).

1. Generally speaking, people who **esteem** themselves are emotionally healthy.

2. When Kevin's essay was **acclaimed** as exemplary, he was thrilled.

3. It is recommended to **laud** false acts of kindness.

4. One way to **venerate** grandparents is to listen to their stories of "the good old days."

5. Praised by all for her genuine and golden heart, Terri was **exalted** to the realm of earth angels.

Lesson 20

ENOUGH IS ENOUGH
Words Relating to More Than Enough

ample copious lavish myriad plethora profuse prolific superfluous surfeit

---

ample (AM-pul) *adj.* abundant; plentiful; enough or more than enough

It will be expensive to send me to college, but my parents have **ample** funds, thank goodness.

or turning in the lost wallet, Heather was given an **ample** reward f $200.

uice and a piece of toast make up an **ample** breakfast for me, lthough Mom thinks I ought to eat more.

ous (KOH-pee-us) *adj.* abundant; much; plentiful

couldn't attend the meeting, so Julie took **copious** notes. Now I know everything that happened there.

The director explained the camp's procedures in **copious** detail, far more than I needed or wanted to know.

It rained **copiously** day and night, leaving the streets flooded.

lavish (LA-vish) (from Lesson 8) *adj.* abundant; in excess

My **lavish** weekend excursion resulted in a huge bill on my dad's Visa card.

Trudy's reaction to the meager furnishings in the dorm room suggests that she's used to more **lavish** living quarters.

On the cruise we ate **lavishly**, enjoying huge meals three times a day and snacks in between.

117

myriad (MIR-ee-ud) *adj.* or *n.* countless; a very large number

Kenny failed the test by making **myriad** mistakes in addition and subtraction.

New York has a **myriad** of restaurants. The number and variety are astounding.

Myriad airplanes filled the sky. It's a wonder they didn't crash into one another.

plethora (PLEH-thuh-ruh) *n.* excess; abundance

The kindergarten room is crowded with a **plethora** of materials and equipment.

There used to be a **plethora** of teachers, but now there is a shortage.

Considering the **plethora** of ways to get lost en route, it's a marvel that you got here so soon.

profuse (pruh-FYOOS) *adj.* abundant; more than enough

Please accept my **profuse** thanks for your hospitality. Your graciousness knows no bounds.

Herman bled so **profusely** from the wound that he almost lost consciousness.

The **profusion** of options in our curriculum gives students many choices to make.

prolific (pruh-LI-fik) *adj.* abundant; producing a great deal; fertile

Despite Marvin's **prolific** fiction writing, he never shared any of his many short stories with others.

A **prolific** artist, Caroline painted hundreds of watercolors and landscapes in her lifetime.

Drew's patience and care in tending to his garden led to a **prolific** harvest of basil, tomatoes, and zucchini.

superfluous (soo-PUR-floo-us) *adj.* overabundant; more than is needed; unnecessary

Since the birthday card was sufficient recognition of the big day, the gift was **superfluous**.

I understood the rules before the race started, so the coach's instructions were **superfluous**.

Most of what I brought along for the camping trip was **superfluous**. I didn't need the majority of it.

surfeit (SUR-fut) *n*. an oversupply

A **surfeit** of donations made the drive to collect more money superfluous.

During Halloween, kids collect a **surfeit** of candy and other sweets.

A **surfeit** of wheat enables the United States to export wheat to needy countries.

MEMORY TIPS

Use these mnemonics (memory devices) to boost your vocabulary. Make up your own memory clues for words in this lesson that are personally challenging. Add these tips—and your own—to your Vocabulary Notebook. One thing you can never get enough of when preparing for the SAT is vocabulary.

copious Let yourself see the word *copies* within **copious**, and think "lots of copies." Certainly "lots of copies" leads to the defining ideas of *abundant* and *plentiful*.

plethora Let the *ple* lead you to *plenty*. When you write **plethora** in your Vocabulary Notebook, underscore *ple* with a colored pen or marker.

superfluous The prefix *super-* means over and above. This knowledge is helpful because superfluous means "above what is needed; extra."

surfeit Like *super-*, *sur-* is also a prefix meaning over and above. So a **surfeit** is an amount over and above what is needed. Using apperception (see Introduction), link a word you most likely already know, surplus, to the new word, **surfeit**. These two-syllable synonyms even have the same number of letters! Solidify the meaning of **surfeit** in your memory.

MATCHING

Match the vocabulary words in Column A with *one or more* of their defining characteristics appearing in Column B.

Column A	Column B
1. surfeit	a. unnecessary
2. myriad	b. big number
3. superfluous	c. glut
4. ample	d. abundant
5. profuse	e. countless

SENTENCE COMPLETION

Remember: Answer choices can be the lesson words themselves, or words that appear in definitions or Memory Tips. Select a word form and part of speech that fit correctly within the sentence.

1. The proud parents _____ their young sons with positive recognition, deserved praise, and packs of collector's edition baseball cards.
   (copious, prolific, surfeit, lavish, ample)

2. With five school-age children, the sensible Coopers made sure that their home was always stocked with _____ school and art supplies.
   (plethora, copious, lavishly, superfluous, fertile)

3. A (an) _____ seamstress, Ms. Petraglia sews several elaborate and finely stitched party dresses each and every week.
   (prolific, profuse, copious, superfluous, ample)

4. _____ books are eagerly waiting for you at the library, where shelves teem with innumerable volumes on every subject and in every genre!
   (Surfeit, Ample, Myriad, Lavish, Superfluous)

5. For Alexandra, a whole grain waffle, orange juice, fresh fruit, and coffee constitute a (an) _____ breakfast; for Alex, pancakes stacked five high, two sausages, and scrambled eggs would be just enough.
(profuse, ample, excess, copious, prolific)

WORDS IN CONTEXT

Based on the context in which each **bold** word is used, identify the word usage of each sentence as either C (Correct) or I (Incorrect).

1. Joanne enjoyed **ample** fineries while camping in the woods.

2. Sasga feels great gratitude for her life, which brims with **profuse** blessings.

3. There are a **plethora** of reasons why I don't wish to go to Europe with you. I can name at least a dozen reasons right off the bat.

4. **Myriad** sleigh riders swept down the snowy hills of Terrace Village; in fact, only two sleighers were spotted.

5. Kurt spoiled his girlfriend with **lavish** gifts of jewelry, handbags, and perfumes.

Review Exercises / Lessons 16–20

VOCABULARY-IN-CONTEXT PARAGRAPH

The paragraph below primarily features words that appear in vocabulary lessons 16–20. For added reinforcement, additional vocabulary words from other lessons may appear in the paragraph. In those cases, the lesson number in which those words appear is indicated within parentheses. In light of the context, the words' meanings should be clear. If you are uncertain about particular meanings, however, take a moment to review the word's definition and illustrative sentences, as provided within the referenced lessons.

Lessons 16–20: School Dance

The *clamor* of the speakers shook the gymnasium floor, and the deejay adjusted the bass with the skill of an *acoustical* engineer. An *exuberant* group of *ebullient* teens dressed in vibrant colors broke out onto the dance floor amid *effervescent* cheers and *strident* calls. Despite the *zealous* pleas of the group, the chaperones *adamantly* refused to permit break-dancing, fearing such raucous behavior could cause a *myriad* of minor injuries to the students. Even so, the students *fervently* enjoyed the music, their friends, and the night. At the end of the electrifying evening, students gave each other high-fives and *vociferously lauded* each others' dance moves while parents *adulated* the chaperones for keeping their children both happy and safe.

NAME THAT CLUSTER

To the left of the groups of words, put the Roman numeral that corresponds with these theme (or cluster) titles:

Words Relating to . . .

  I. Being Stubborn
 II. Enthusiasm and Passion
III. More Than Enough
 IV. Sound
  V. Praise and Respect

Cluster Title _____ 1. mellifluous, acoustics, euphony, vociferous, discordant

Cluster Title _____ 2. avid, zealous, effervescent, ardent, fervent

Cluster Title _____ 3. laud, revere, venerate, extol, eulogize

Cluster Title _____ 4. obdurate, hidebound, obstinate, adamant, unwavering

Cluster Title _____ 5. lavish, myriad, copious, plethora, profuse

---

SENTENCE COMPLETION

Note: On the new SAT (March 2016 and forward), multiple-choice sentence completion questions have been eliminated. However, sentence completion questions remain in this book as a vocabulary-strengthening exercise. Make flashcards for the words that are unknown or unfamiliar to you.

Read the sentence through carefully. Then from the five vocabulary words given in parentheses, circle the word that fits *best*.

1. The grandchildren _____ Grandfather Albert not only for his infinite wisdom, but also for his family loyalty.
(lavished, hidebound, venerated, effervesced, impassioned)

2. Jumping up and down joyfully, Miranda became increasingly _____ as she won one terrific raffle prize after another!
(ebullient, fanatical, superficial, copious, strident)

3. Donna's _____ voice has a calming effect on the people she talks to.
(plethora, vibrant, exuberant, mellifluous, surfeit)

4. At the charity dinner, the _____ of the loudspeaker made it nearly impossible to have a conversation with the person sitting next to you.
(recalcitrant, fervent, dogged, din, adulation)

5. A (An) _____ coin collector, Connie has coins from nearly every country around the world.
(clamorous, acoustical, cacophonous, avid, esteemed)

6. To Susan's sensitive ear, the harpsichord sounds harsh and
_____, whereas the piano sounds wonderfully _____.
copious...fervent
discordant...mellifluous
unyielding...obstinate
acoustical...vociferous
effervescent...ebullient

7. You can try to persuade me with _____ gifts, but I remain
_____; I simply will *never* be able to see your point of view
on this issue.
myriad...vibrant
venerated...clamorous
lavish...obstinate
euphonious...strident
superfluous...exuberant

8. Wide-eyed and garrulous, the children were _____ upon
seeing the shiny sea lions and majestic pelicans cavorting in their
natural habitat!
(exuberant, superfluous, laudatory, discordant, willful)

9. Trying to sell anything from straw hats to shell necklaces to henna
tattoos, _____ vendors flooded "Hound Alley" as the family made its way along the cobble pathway, thick with vendors, to
Chileno Beach.
(acoustical, panegyric, euphonious, myriad, mellifluous)

10. Because Ruth writes with a (an) _____ of detailed descrip-
tions, readers find it difficult to follow her storyline, tending to get
lost in the _____ particulars.
mellifluousness...unwavering
surfeit...profuse
resolve...intractable
din...vociferous
accolade...exalted

ONE DOESN'T BELONG

Three of the words in each grouping relate to each other somehow. Cross off the one word that does not belong with the others. For a challenge, write the word that does not belong on the line below, and try your best to define that word. *Note:* Some of the words have been taken from definitions or exercises that appear within the lessons.

1. vivacious   vibrant   vitality   vociferous

   _____ means _____

2. dogged   effervescent   resolved   inflexible

   _____ means _____

3. copious   defiant   profuse   plethoric

   _____ means _____

4. recalcitrant   cacophonous   strident   din

   _____ means _____

5. extol   surfeit   panegyrize   esteem

   _____ means _____

Lesson 21

MMMmmm . . . DELICIOUS!
Words Relating to Food and Hunger

> **abstemious alimentary culinary delectable emaciated epicurean glutton palatable ravenous savory sustenance voracious**

abstemious (ab-STEE-mee-us) *adj.* holding back from eating or drinking too much

Grandpa eats like a bird. Mother fears that his **abstemious** nature may not be good for him.

With a buffet dinner that includes an Italian hero and pepperoni pizza, it is hard to be **abstemious**.

I need the willpower to be more **abstemious** if I'm going to lose 10 pounds by June.

alimentary (a-luh-MEN-tree) *adj.* relating to food and nourishment

Fast foods provide little nourishment, but fresh fruits and vegetables are good for your **alimentary** health.

In biology we learned about the **alimentary** canal, the system in the body for swallowing and digesting food.

I saw an interesting program about nutrition, digestion, and other **alimentary** matters.

culinary (KUH-luh-ner-ee) *adj.* having to do with cooking, preparing meals

Our chef went to the **Culinary** Institute to learn all about food preparation.

Airline food is anything but a **culinary** delight.

Martha was distressed about how awful the dinner was. She called it "a **culinary** disaster."

delectable (dih-LEK-tuh-bul) *adj.* delicious

The aroma of fresh-baked bread and other **delectable**, mouth-watering foods wafted through the house.

For Gary, there's no more **delectable** meal than baked macaroni and cheese.

When asked, "How's the roast beef?" Meg replied, "**Delectable**," as gravy ran down her chin.

emaciated (ih-MAY-shee-ay-tid) *adj.* very, very thin due to lack of adequate food; terribly undernourished

Winter out on the range with very little food left the cattle **emaciated**.

Anorexia left Tina looking **emaciated**, like a victim of malnutrition.

It is heartbreaking to look at photos of **emaciated** children who are victims of famine.

epicurean (eh-pih-kyoo-REE-un) *adj.* having to do with relishing the pleasure of eating and drinking (*n.* epicure)

At the reception, the table was piled high with the most delicious **epicurean** delights.

A McDonald's cheeseburger and fries may taste good to some people, but it is not my idea of an **epicurean** meal.

As a die-hard **epicure**, Clyde eats at only the very best restaurants.

glutton (GLUH-tn) *n.* one who overindulges in food and drink

Eddie proved he was a **glutton** by eating a whole pumpkin pie and a half-gallon of ice cream at one sitting.

Rachel was such a **glutton**, she ate huge chipotle burritos even when she wasn't hungry.

I don't eat much candy, but I become a **glutton** in front of a plate of chocolate chip cookies!

palatable (PA-luh-tuh-bul) *adj.* pleasing to the taste buds

This stew tastes awful. To make it more **palatable**, add salt and garlic.

Zina found Ethan's rabbit stew **unpalatable** and refused to eat it.

Which do you find more **palatable**, shrimp or lobster?

ravenous (RA-vuh-nus) *adj*. very hungry

A day spent outdoors makes me **ravenous** enough to eat a hippopotamus.

Matt is a **ravenous** eater. When he's not poking around in the refrigerator, he's exploring the pantry for snacks.

Caviar is supposedly a gourmet food, but I'd have to be **ravenous** before swallowing fish eggs.

savory (SAY-vuh-ree) *adj*. tasty or good smelling

Spices can turn a bland, tasteless dish into a **savory** one.

Don't gulp the wine as though it's a glass of soda. To **savor** it, sip slowly.

The label on the can says the soup is **savory**, but to me it has no flavor whatsoever.

sustenance (SUS-tuh-nens) *n*. nourishment and related provisions that sustain life; nourishment; one's livelihood

Bread, pasta, rice, and various other grains form a primary **sustenance** for many cultures throughout the world.

Lean protein and fresh vegetables provide healthful **sustenance** for human beings.

Sabrina's daily **sustenance** includes reading an inspirational passage each morning from a periodical to which she subscribes.

voracious (vuh-RAY-shus) *adj*. greedy; gluttonous; ravenous; insatiable

Because Molly skipped breakfast and lunch, she had a **voracious** appetite at dinner.

Tucker is a **voracious** eater. Every day he polishes off a half-dozen hamburgers, a pound of potato salad, and a giant bowl of chocolate mousse.

Sally reads mysteries **voraciously**. No sooner does she finish one than she starts reading another.

MEMORY TIPS

Use these mnemonics (memory devices) to boost your vocabulary. Make up your own memory clues for words in this lesson that are personally challenging. Add these tips—and your own—to your Vocabulary Notebook. Remember, vocabulary building is key to increasing your score on the verbal SAT.

alimentary Recall your classwork in biology and life science. Have you heard of the "alimentary canal"? If so, link your knowledge to the meaning of **alimentary**, pertaining to food and nourishment. According to Britannica online, the **alimentary canal** is the "pathway along which food travels when it is eaten and from which solid wastes are expelled." The **alimentary** canal includes the mouth, pharynx, esophagus, stomach, small and large intestines, and the anal canal.

<u>del</u>**ectable** Let the sound and look of this word help you remember its meaning. After all, there's quite a resemblance between **delectable** and two of its synonyms, *delicious* and *delightful*. All three terms begin with *del* and they are similar—if not the same—in length. Write <u>del</u>ectable, <u>del</u>icious, and <u>del</u>ightful as a mini-cluster in your Vocabulary Notebook.

glutton Did you know that *glut* means "an oversupply or surplus"? If so, then your preexisting knowledge will help you remember the meaning of **glutton**, a person who indulges in a *glut*, or oversupply, of food and drink.

palatable Think "pleasing to the palate," the roof of the mouth. Do not confuse with *palpable* (Lesson 36).

MATCHING

Match the vocabulary words in Column A with *one or more* of their defining characteristics appearing in Column B.

Column A	Column B
1. emaciated	a. greedily hungry
2. alimentary	b. an overeater
3. savory	c. extremely skinny
4. ravenous	d. having to do with cooking
5. culinary	e. having to do with nutritional needs
6. glutton	f. tasty

SENTENCE COMPLETION

Remember: Answer choices can be the lesson words themselves, or words that appear in definitions or Memory Tips. Select a word form and part of speech that fit correctly within the sentence.

1. The _____ raccoons knocked over our garbage cans and ate every last morsel of our leftover pizza, mozzarella sticks, and garlic knots.
   (savory, emaciated, alimentary, gluttony, ravenous)

2. _____ when it comes to Italian food especially, Gideon ate a pound of rigatoni, seven meatballs, one whole sausage, and two servings of tricolor salad at his midday meal.
   (Savory, Palatable, Epicurean, Abstemious, Gluttonous)

3. To make the baby back pork ribs more _____, Gail basted them in a mixture of finger-lickin' barbecue sauce, ketchup, and Jamaican spices, then topped them with a homemade pineapple-peach salsa.
   (emaciated, voracious, savory, ravenous, unpalatable)

4. To become a premier chef, one must not only have _____ skill but also a visual aesthetic, coupled with gastronomic creativity.
   (delectable, culinary, abstemious, gluttonous, ravenous)

5. Since Hannah knew she would indulge in her favorite chocolate mousse birthday cake over the weekend, this figure-conscious birthday girl remained rather _____ throughout the week.
(voracious, palatable, delectable, abstemious, epicurean)

WORDS IN CONTEXT

Based on the context in which each **bold** word is used, identify the word usage of each sentence as either C (Correct) or I (Incorrect).

1. **Voracious** Victor just picked at mealtimes.

2. Reading and writing are **alimentary** subjects for any first-grade student.

3. The **gluttonous** guest ate the entire loaf of fresh-baked bread herself.

4. Surviving on celery sticks and rice cakes, Emma became increasingly **emaciated**.

5. The **savory** aroma attracted passersby to the new Town Bakery.

Lesson 22

EASY DOES IT
Words Relating to Being Careful

chary circumspect conscientious exacting gingerly
heedful meticulous scrupulous vigilant wary

---

chary (CHAIR-ee) *adj.* cautious; wary

Be **chary** about what you say about others. You don't know who may be listening.

Where pickpockets ply their trade, it pays to be **chary** of where you keep your purse or wallet.

Chary of burglars, we set our security alarm whenever we go out.

circumspect (SUR-km-spekt) *adj.* careful and cautious before acting

Myra is too personally involved in the case to be **circumspect** about it.

Be **circumspect** when choosing a college. Don't get carried away by your emotions.

Kevin contributes less to class discussions than most other students do, but his thoughtful comments reveal his **circumspection**.

conscientious (kahn-shee-EN-shus) *adj.* relating to doing what one knows is right; scrupulous

Marta was promoted twice for her **conscientious** performance on the job. No one works harder than she does.

You've made a **conscientious** effort to clean the basement, but it's still filthy despite all your hard work.

Tino pumps iron **conscientiously**, at least three times a day for half an hour.

exacting (ig-ZAK-ting) *adj*. requiring a great deal of care or effort; painstaking

The lacrosse coach's standards were so **exacting** that it was hard to achieve them.

It's **exacting** work to build a stereo from a kit. If you are careless, the stereo won't work.

Kyra loves to make tiny pins and brooches, but Kara doesn't have the patience to do such **exacting** work.

gingerly (JIN-jer-lee) *adj*. very carefully

Because Sue **gingerly** placed the sleeping baby in his crib, the infant didn't wake up.

Build a house of cards **gingerly**. One careless move will make it collapse.

Pet the kitty **gingerly**, or you may hurt it.

heedful (HEED-ful) *adj*. paying careful attention to

If the novice skier had **heeded** the signs, he wouldn't have found himself on the expert slope.

Be **heedful** of your counselor's advice. His experience is worth a lot when you apply to college.

It's smart to **heed** the instructions before operating a chain saw.

meticulous (muh-TIH-kyoo-lus) *adj*. very careful; fussy; finicky; fastidious

A **meticulous** carpenter, Emil makes perfect joints and dovetails, even better than a machine does.

Her makeup is **meticulously** applied. Eyeliner, lipstick, blush—no one puts them on as carefully as Lisa.

During surgery, the incision is kept **meticulously** clean to reduce the possibility of infection.

scrupulous (SKROO-pyoo-lus) *adj*. showing great care and honesty, based on personal belief of what is right and proper

Jade is **scrupulous** about doing her own work. She won't even let a classmate proofread her papers.

He's as **scrupulous** a politician as you can find anywhere. There's not a hint of scandal in his long career.

Follow the rules of the contest **scrupulously**, or you may be disqualified.

vigilant (VI-juh-lunt) *adj.* carefully alert and watchful

The driving instructor told his students, "When switching lanes, always look for other cars. **Vigilance** is the price of safety."

Mrs. Trueport **vigilantly** watched the tots playing in the backyard. She didn't take her eyes off them all afternoon.

Ever since Terry fell into a pothole, Dad has been more **vigilant** about keeping the driveway in good repair.

wary (WAIR-ee) *adj.* cautious, careful

If the ship's captain had been more **wary** of storms, he never would have put to sea and lost his ship that day.

Be **wary** of offers that sound too good to be true; they may contain a hidden trap.

We were told to be **wary** of other students who talk even in jest about bringing a gun to school.

MEMORY TIPS

Use these mnemonics (memory devices) to boost your vocabulary. Make up your own memory clues for words in this lesson that are particularly challenging for you. Add these tips—and your own—to your Vocabulary Notebook. Remember, increasing your vocabulary can help you score higher on the verbal section of the SAT.

chary, wary Learn these two SAT-level synonyms as a rhyming pair—can't get much easier than that!

circumspect This word is a blend of the prefix, *circum-*, and the root, *spec*. *Circum-* means *around* (as in a geometry term you might know, circumference). *Spec* means *seeing* (as in spectator and inspect). In other words, **circumspect** means *looking around*—or being cautious and watchful before making decisions or taking action.

vigilant Write this word in your Vocabulary Notebook, and make the dots of the two *i*'s into "watchful" and "alert" human eyes! Once you sketch *eyes* in place of the dots, this memory clue becomes a word-picture clue. Word pictures are very appealing to visual learners, and they tend to stick.

As a noun, a **vigil** is a *night watch*. For example: Since her son had a high fever, the mother kept a **vigil** at his bedside.

wary You know what it means to be a*war*e. Link this preexisting knowledge to **wary**. Both words share the letter cluster *war*. Remember that **wary** and **chary** are SAT synonyms that sound alike!

MATCHING

Match the vocabulary words in Column A with *one or more* of their defining characteristics appearing in Column B.

Column A	Column B
1. vigilant	a. attentive to detail
2. wary	b. conducting oneself based on a sense of right versus wrong
3. meticulous	c. requiring great effort
4. exacting	d. wide-eyed; alert
5. gingerly	e. very carefully
6. heedful	f. listening to advice or warnings
7. scrupulous	g. fussy
8. circumspect	h. careful, cautious

SENTENCE COMPLETION

Remember: *Answer choices can be the lesson words themselves, or words that appear in definitions or Memory Tips. Select a word form and part of speech that fit correctly within the sentence.*

1. Barbara is so _____ about coordinating her outfits that everything has to match impeccably, from handbag to belt to shoes to scarf.
   (gingerly, heedful, meticulous, chary, vigilant)

2. Speak to the baby softly and hold him _____, since loud sounds and abrupt movements may shock him and make him cry.
   (circumspectly, painstakingly, vigilantly, heedfully, gingerly)

3. A _____ work ethic will bring you personal gratification and success; clients appreciate good old-fashioned effort, honesty, and reliability.
   (gingerly, finicky, inspecting, vigilant, scrupulous)

4. _____ about her personal safety, Janine refrained from shopping after dark.
   (Chary, Exacting, Scrupulous, Painstaking, Fastidious)

5. Encouraging his driver's education students to be _____ when in the driver's seat, instructor Eugene, who was serious as well as humorous, told his students to look for "Marvin the Midget" over their shoulders before backing up and to be watchful for "Pedestrian Patty" before crossing through intersections.
   (vigilant, scrupulous, finicky, conscientiously, heeded)

WORDS IN CONTEXT

Based on the context in which each **bold** word is used, identify the word usage of each sentence as either C (Correct) or I (Incorrect).

1. **Wary** about her surroundings, Leana always looks over her shoulder when walking the narrow streets of her neighborhood.

2. The **circumspect** of the three-dimensional figure was hard to measure.

3. Gus's **gingerly** sense of humor made him the life of every party.

4. A **scrupulous** and honest handyman, Lee makes sure that every home repair is done efficiently and thoroughly. Client satisfaction is Lee's main goal.

5. Walking across an outdoor tightrope on a windy day is an **exacting** feat.

HERE TODAY, GONE TOMORROW...

Words Relating to Being Short-Lived in Time or Place

ephemeral evanescent fleeting itinerant nomadic peripatetic
transient transitory volatile

---

ephemeral (ih-FEM-rul) *adj.* lasting a short time; fleeting

Jodi's romances are usually **ephemeral**. She just skips from one boy to another.

Dave has followed baseball steadily since he was nine, but his interest in other sports has been **ephemeral**.

To a child, time goes by slowly—but to an old man, time is **ephemeral**.

evanescent (eh-vuh-NEH-snt) *adj.* vanishing quickly; fleeting

Snowfall in spring is usually **evanescent**. The snow melts very quickly.

The rumor is that an **evanescent** ghost haunts the forest. People who've seen it say that it vanishes as suddenly as it appears.

Old timers tend to lament the **evanescence** of youth. "How quickly youth passes," they say.

fleeting (FLEE-ting) *adj.* short-lived

Willie and Wanda had a **fleeting** romance. Their fling couldn't have lasted more than 24 hours.

Time is **fleeting** when you are enjoying yourself, while pain seems to last forever.

The first sign of trouble was a **fleeting** pain in my stomach that couldn't have lasted for more than a second or two.

itinerant (eye-TIH-nuh-runt) *adj*. wandering about; tending to move around, travel

Susan and Ellie wandered around Europe for months, enjoying a carefree, **itinerant** life.

I rarely see my **itinerant** uncle. He's a globe-hopper, constantly on the move.

Peter's **itinerary** for two weeks included stops in 10 cities and five countries.

nomadic (no-MA-dik) *adj*. wandering

Nomadic tribes wandered endlessly around the land.

Oren, like a **nomad**, cannot settle down in one place. He has to keep moving.

Nomadic people who lack permanent homes are often called gypsies.

peripatetic (per-uh-puh-TEH-tik) *adj*. moving or walking about; itinerant

During his lecture, the teacher paced **peripatetically** around the room. The constant movement distracted me from what he was saying.

Here today, gone tomorrow—that's the kind of **peripatetic** life Carl enjoys.

Lila was exhausted after a **peripatetic** shopping trip to the city. She had walked from store to store all day long.

transient (TRAN-shee-unt) *adj*. lasting for only a short time; temporary

The motel serves a **transient** clientele. Few visitors stay for more than a night.

The large number of houses up for sale in this neighborhood suggests that the population here is **transient**.

The students are **transients** in a school. They stay for a few years and then leave; the teachers, however, remain in place.

transitory (TRAN-suh-tawr-ee) *adj.* fleeting

> On her 100th birthday, Aunt Thalia reflected, "Youth is a **transitory** time of life, while growing old is a more permanent condition."

> The morning fog is **transitory**. It always burns off by midday.

> The joy of winning a game is a **transitory** feeling; it lasts only until the next game.

volatile (VAH-luh-tl) *adj.* explosive or changing very quickly

> Mia and Greg are a **volatile** couple. One heated argument and their relationship is history.

> Lou can turn angry in an instant. He has a **volatile** temper.

> Careful where you store that can. It contains **volatile** fuel that blows up when heated.

MEMORY TIPS

Use these mnemonics (memory devices) to boost your vocabulary. Make up your own memory clues for words in this lesson that are personally challenging. Add these tips—and your own—to your Vocabulary Notebook.

evanescent Let the sound of *vanesc*, the underlined part of this word, remind you of *vanishing*, the essential meaning of this SAT word. Again, this memory technique works by linking what you most likely already know (vanishing) to something new (**evanescent**).

transient, transitory Both of these words share the prefix *trans-*, which has to do with movement across. Additional words containing *trans* include transportation, transmit, and translucent.

volatile Because the adjective **volatile** means "explosive; changeable," say "Volatile volcano!" three times in a row. This chant will help to solidify the meaning of the explosive vocabulary word **volatile**. "Volatile volcano! Volatile volcano! Volatile volcano!"

MATCHING

Match the vocabulary words in Column A with *one or more* of their defining characteristics appearing in Column B.

Column A

1. ephemeral
2. transient
3. evanescent
4. volatile
5. peripatetic

Column B

a. explosive
b. traveling about
c. vanishing
d. walking around a lot
e. short-lived

SENTENCE COMPLETION

Remember: Answer choices can be the lesson words themselves, or words that appear in definitions or Memory Tips. Select a word form and part of speech that fit correctly within the sentence.

1. No longer needing to migrate to find their food, early humans became less _____ with the onset of agriculture and an increase in technology, which allowed them to stay in one place for a longer period of time.
   (nomadic, fleeting, volatile, evanescent, ephemeral)

2. Junior high school is shorter than elementary school and high school; these middle years of school are truly _____.
   (fleetingly, peripatetic, volatile, translucent, transitory)

3. When I was a child, time used to move as slowly as lightning bugs drift in the summer evening skies; now that I am an adult, time is _____, passing by like a shooting star.
   (volatility, nomadic, ephemeral, transmitting, peripatetic)

4. If _____ substances are not stored precisely according to the written instructions on their product labels, there is a significant risk of combustion!
   (itinerant, translucent, nomadic, volatile, fleeting)

5. My cousin is truly a (an) _____; throughout the year, he lives in many different places, such as Brazil, Mexico, and Fire Island, New York.
   (itinerant, ephemeral, fleeing, transitory, nomadic)

WORDS IN CONTEXT

Based on the context in which each **bold** word is used, identify the word usage of each sentence as either C (Correct) or I (Incorrect).

1. People who like change prefer a **nomadic** lifestyle.

2. Sheila's junior year of college was an **itinerant** one; she traveled to and studied in seven major European cities in nine months.

3. For Jesse, contentment was merely **transitory**. Unfortunately, he rarely could manage to stay happy for more than 72 hours.

4. A **volatile** temperament is a highly individualistic one.

5. One might call "momentary lapses of confusion" **ephemeral**.

Lesson 24

OLD HAT, NEW HAT?
Words Relating to the Old or the New

> antediluvian antiquated antiquity archaic obsolete relic
> contemporary inception innovation novel unprecedented

The Old . . .

antediluvian (an-tih-duh-LOO-vee-un) *adj.* very, very old; antiquated

The shop contains **antediluvian** machines that ought to be replaced with up-to-date equipment.

That joke about the chicken crossing the road is **antediluvian**. Can't you think of a more current one?

You can buy that farmhouse for a song because it's **antediluvian**. It even uses gas instead of electricity for lighting.

antiquated (AN-tuh-kway-tud) *adj.* very old and no longer in use; obsolete

The proverbial housewife standing over a hot stove all day is an **antiquated** stereotype rarely seen anymore.

Some of our history textbooks are **antiquated** and full of outdated information.

The author says he prefers to write on an **antiquated** portable typewriter instead of a computer.

antiquity (an-TIH-kwuh-tee) *n.* ancient times

Antiquity usually refers to times prior to the Middle Ages.

Hippocrates articulated a code of medical ethics that is as valid today as it was in **antiquity**.

Lord Elgin stole sculptures from sites of **antiquity** in Greece and put them in London's British Museum.

archaic (ar-KAY-ik) *adj*. old; from a much earlier time; antiquated

Some scholars study **archaic** languages no longer spoken anywhere in the world.

Footnotes are used to explain **archaic** terms known to Shakespeare's audience but not to modern readers.

Some glassmakers use contemporary methods, but most Venetian workshops still rely on **archaic** techniques.

obsolete (ahb-suh-LEET) *adj*. old; outdated, no longer in use

My dad has a shelf full of **obsolete** phonograph records containing some of the same music I have on CDs.

In the business world, where everything is stored on computers, filing cabinets full of paper records have become **obsolete**.

Although rotary-dial phones are **obsolete**, our family still uses one for old time's sake.

relic (REH-lik) *n*. a custom or object that has been around for a very, very long time

Fritzi's spinning wheel is a **relic** that's been in the family for generations.

The museum displays **relics** of ancient cultures from all over the world.

In some ways Aunt Henrietta seems like a **relic** from the past, but she can quote you the latest rap lyrics verbatim.

The New . . .

contemporary (kun-TEM-puh-rer-ee) *adj*. modern, new; relating to the same time period

The course is called ***Contemporary*** *Civilization*, but much of it is devoted to the study of ancient history.

Radiant heat, instead of traditional forced air or steam heat, is becoming the standard in **contemporary** buildings.

Although my art teacher is pretty old, she encourages us to paint in **contemporary** styles.

inception (in-SEP-shun) *n.* the start, the beginning of something

Since the **inception** of computers, the library has become a swinging place.

The **inception** of e-mail has cut the use of postage stamps and envelopes.

The cost of paper has skyrocketed, however, since the **inception** of courses in desktop publishing.

innovation (ih-nuh-VAY-shun) *n.* something new

The coach has instituted an **innovation** in our training. Instead of running ten laps twice a day, he has us running two laps ten times a day.

The company makes **innovative** water filters that can add fresh lemon flavor to tap water.

Gehry's buildings are always **innovative**. No architect has ever designed structures quite like his.

novel (NAH-vul) *adj.* new

Few other books group vocabulary words according to themes. Barron's believes that the **novel** format of this book will give you an edge when preparing for the SAT.

Serving kids steamed vegetables for breakfast: now that's a **novel** diet!

A conch shell made into a nightlight is the souvenir shop's best-selling **novelty**.

unprecedented (un-PREH-suh-den-tud) *adj.* novel; unparalleled

The number of delayed flights is **unprecedented**. Never before have so many travelers arrived so late to their destinations.

Giving students money instead of grades for their achievement is **unprecedented** and will never be accepted by the community.

The heat wave this summer is **unprecedented**. There's never been a summer as hot as this one.

MEMORY TIPS

Use these mnemonics (memory devices) to boost your vocabulary. Make up your own memory clues for words in this lesson that are challenging for you. Add these tips—and your own—to your Vocabulary Notebook.

antiquated, **antiquity** Like previous memory tips, this one works by linking something you already know to something new. In this case, you most likely know *antique*. Since an *antique* is commonly referred to as something that dates back 100 years or more, link this knowledge to the words **antiquated** and **antiquity**, both having to do with being *very, very* old.

novel, **innovation** Learn the word root *nova* to help you remember these words and others. *Nova* is a root that means *new*. Additional words containing the root *nova* include novice, novelty, and renovate.

Word roots *neo* and *nou* also mean *new*. Words containing these roots include **neophyte** (beginner, rookie, novice), **neonate** (newborn), and **nouveau riche** (a person who has recently become rich).

MATCHING

Match the vocabulary words in Column A with *one or more* of their defining characteristics appearing in Column B.

Column A	Column B
1. relic	a. very, very old
2. obsolete	b. relating to present time
3. novel	c. an invention
4. innovation	d. the very beginning
5. antediluvian	e. a very old object
6. inception	f. outdated; no longer used
7. contemporary	g. original

SENTENCE COMPLETION

Remember: Answer choices can be the lesson words themselves, or words that appear in definitions or Memory Tips. Select a word form and part of speech that fit correctly within the sentence.

1. Unlike the English cottage style of home decorating, which has been called comfy and quaint, the _____ style of décor has been described as modern, sleek, and simple.
   (novel, unprecedented, relic, antediluvian, contemporary)

2. Some people consider eight-track tapes, LP records, and manual typewriters to be _____, while antique dealers regard them as collector's items.
   (inception, innovation, relics, neonates, novel)

3. Although Grandma is almost 90, she is hip and mentally keen; there is nothing _____ about her, except for the brooch she wears that was given to her by her great-grandmother!
   (contemporary, neophyte, innovative, antediluvian, unparalleled)

4. As more and more people pay their bills electronically and online, writing out checks every month is slowly becoming a (an) _____ practice.
   (obsolete, contemporary, inception, antiquity, novel)

5. Modern American poet e. e. cummings has such an unconventional writing and punctuation style that when his poems were first published, critics undoubtedly remarked how unique and _____ his literary technique was.
   (relic, antiquated, unprecedented, archaic, antediluvian)

WORDS IN CONTEXT

Based on the context in which each **bold** word is used, determine if the word usage is either C (Correct) or I (Incorrect).

1. Banging coconuts together makes for an **antiquated** percussive instrument.

2. You could say that **contemporary** thinkers are "with the times."

3. Jerry adores artwork that has withstood the ages. He frequently shops at "The **Inception** Connection."

4. Michelangelo's masterful paintings and sculptures are practically **antediluvian**, for they have been around since the 16th century.

5. Mrs. Wath is an **innovative** teacher. She has been using the same teaching methods and supplies for the past 30 years.

Lesson 25

IS ANYBODY THERE? IS ANYTHING THERE?

Words Relating to Being Sneaky or Hardly Noticeable

clandestine covert furtive inconspicuous sly stealthy
surreptitious unobtrusive

---

clandestine (klan-DES-tun) *adj.* hidden, secret, concealed

During the party, Gia and Jason stole away into the woods for a **clandestine** rendezvous.

It was important to keep the operation **clandestine** to protect our undercover agents.

Hanssen revealed the FBI's **clandestine** plan to build a tunnel under the Russian embassy in Washington.

covert (KOH-vurt) *adj.* secret, hidden

The administration's **covert** plan to overthrow the rebel leader failed because top secret government documents fell into the wrong hands.

Gerry **covertly** transferred funds from the company to his own bank account, but an investigator uncovered Gerry's crime.

Under cover of darkness, the workers slipped **covertly** across the border.

furtive (FUR-tiv) *adj.* sneaky

Jane and Henry didn't know that I observed them exchanging **furtive** glances in biology class.

Knowing that Grandma would disapprove, Robbie **furtively** grabbed a handful of cookies when she wasn't looking.

Before Ben stole a **furtive** peek at Marge's answer sheet, he made sure no one was looking.

inconspicuous (in-kun-SPIH-kyoo-wus) *adj*. hardly noticeable

The birthmark on Lilly's cheek was noticeable at birth, but as she grew older it became more and more **inconspicuous**.

Despite her flaming red hair and a figure that usually made heads turn, she remained **inconspicuous** throughout the evening.

Because the bandit made the mistake of wearing a **conspicuous** red hat during the holdup, he was arrested almost immediately.

sly (SLIE) *adj*. underhanded, furtive

Using a **sly** line of questions, Ben tricked the witness into revealing the true story.

All summer Jojo played pool on the **sly**. By September no one realized how skillful he'd become.

At the candy counter, Cal reached for a candy bar and **slyly** stuffed it into his pocket.

stealthy (STEL-thee) *adj*. secretive, sly

The airplane known as the **Stealth** Bomber lives up to its name by eluding radar detection.

It's the story of a **stealthy** man who breaks into suburban homes but doesn't steal anything. He just gets his kicks that way.

Using **stealth**, the Navy SEALs avoided detection and blew up the enemy ship.

surreptitious (sur-up-TIH-shus) *adj*. done or made in a secret, stealthy way

Using **surreptitious** methods, the terrorists planted a time bomb in the railway station. Fortunately, the device was found before it could explode.

William's **surreptitious** behavior has me worried. He's up to something sneaky, I'm sure.

During the test, Damian **surreptitiously** studied the answer sheet he had taped to the palm of his hand.

unobtrusive (un-ub-TROO-siv) *adj*. inconspicuous; not easily noticed

There was nothing **unobtrusive** about Tina's diamond earrings; they were the size of golf balls.

Sophie hates being noticed, so she wears the most **unobtrusive** clothes imaginable.

The table stood **unobtrusively** in the corner for years until Aunt Rhoda noticed it was a valuable antique.

MEMORY TIPS

Use these mnemonics (memory devices) to boost your vocabulary. Make up your own memory clues for words in this lesson that are personally challenging. Add these tips—and your own—to your Vocabulary Notebook. Vocabulary is at the heart of this test.

<u>covert</u> Think *covered* when you see this word. As the definition tells you, **covert** means *hidden* or *secret*. Now certainly *covered* relates to this word's definition. In fact, in some sentences the contextual meaning of **covert** could simply mean *covered*.

<u>inconspicuous</u> It is helpful to know the root word *spic* (also *spec*) in order to commit this word to your memory. *Spic* has to do with *seeing*. (Think of these words: <u>spic</u>tacle, <u>spec</u>tator, in<u>spec</u>t). As you might already know, the prefix *con-* (and *com-*) means *with* or *together*. In this particular word, the first prefix in this word, *in-*, means *not*. So, linking the prefixes and roots together, **inconspicuous** more or less means "not with seeing." There you have it; **inconspicuous** means *hardly noticeable*.

<u>stealthy</u> Have you heard of "stealth" aircraft? By using special materials and designs that either absorb or don't reflect radar waves well, they can fly right over the target and still remain virtually undetectable on radar, showing up (if at all) as something the size of a large bird.

SENTENCE COMPLETION

Remember: *Answer choices can be the lesson words themselves, or words that appear in definitions or Memory Tips. Select a word form and part of speech that fit correctly within the sentence.*

1. "Closet eaters" can be called _____ eaters, since they do not want anyone to see them indulging in brownies and Snickers bars. (unobtrusive, conspicuous, spectacle, covert, obtrusive)

2. Hoping to get her kids to eat healthier, Mom _____ slipped pureed carrots and onions into their chicken noodle soup, hoping the secret ingredients would be undetected.
(conspicuously, surreptitiously, obtrusively, sly, furtiveness)

3. Always wanting to treat others when they dined out for lunch, Auntie Lil, _____ as could be, stuck a $20 bill into my purse every time, without my even knowing.
(slyly, conspicuously, clandestine, inspecting, stealth)

4. Even though the birthmark is smack in the middle of the bridge of my nose, it's very faint and therefore _____.
(obtrusive, sly, inconspicuous, covert, clandestine)

5. The private investigator assured us that the most _____ techniques would be used in order to carry out his latest _____ undercover project.
(spectacle...sly, stealthy...covert, conspicuous....unobtrusive, furtive...spectator, obtrusive...stealth)

WORDS IN CONTEXT

Based on the context in which each **bold** word is used, identify the word usage of each sentence as either C (Correct) or I (Incorrect).

1. **Covert** activities are public knowledge.

2. Wearing an oversized hat and with long hair hanging over her face, Dawn was obviously trying to make herself **inconspicuous**.

3. Luke **furtively** made his phone calls to Jessica since he knew his parents did not approve of his latest girlfriend.

4. A **sly** trick is one that all are meant to understand.

5. Janet and Mark kept their hand-holding **clandestine** since they wanted the world to know their affection for one another.

Review Exercises / Lessons 21–25

VOCABULARY-IN-CONTEXT PARAGRAPH

The paragraph below primarily features words that appear in vocabulary lessons 21–25. For added reinforcement, additional vocabulary words from other lessons may appear in the paragraph. In those cases, the lesson number in which those words appear is indicated within parentheses. In light of the context, the words' meanings should be clear. If you are uncertain about particular meanings, however, take a moment to review the word's definition and illustrative sentences, as provided within the referenced lessons.

Lessons 21–25: The Magical Gourmet

Every Wednesday morning, the *voracious* masses gathered *surreptitiously* around the *antiquated* fountain in town square, in anticipation of the Magical Gourmet. The *peripatetic epicurean* would arrive at noon to conjure up his *delectable* concoctions. *Stealthily*, he plucked *savory* spices from an *archaic* leather pouch which hung from his shoulder. Next, he *gingerly* tossed a handful of fresh herbs into an *antediluvian* black crock pot. With a final flourish, he *furtively* added a final *covert* ingredient. Then, after he quietly chanted a few *enigmatic* (Lesson 10) words, the *delectable* lunch was fully prepared. The *ravenous* crowd enjoyed the meal and ate until they were *satiated*.

NAME THAT CLUSTER

To the left of the groups of words, put the Roman numeral that corresponds with these theme (or cluster) titles:

Words Relating to . . .

   I. Being Careful
  II. The Old or the New
 III. Food and Hunger
 IV. Being Sneaky or Hardly Noticeable
  V. Being Short-Lived in Time or Place

Cluster Title _____ 1. sly, surreptitious, stealthy, inconspicuous, unobtrusive

Cluster Title _____ 2. archaic, novel, innovative, antediluvian, obsolete

Cluster Title _____ 3. voracious, alimentary, savory, palatable, emaciated

Cluster Title _____ 4. transient, peripatetic, nomadic, itinerant, ephemeral

Cluster Title _____ 5. chary, conscientious, heedful, scrupulous, wary

---

SENTENCE COMPLETION

Note: On the new SAT (March 2016 and forward), multiple-choice sentence completion questions have been eliminated. However, sentence completion questions remain in this book as a vocabulary-strengthening exercise. Make flashcards for the words that are unknown or unfamiliar to you.

Read the sentence through carefully. Then from the five vocabulary words given in parentheses, circle the word that fits *best*.

1. In the past five years, the Delsons have lived in the United States, Switzerland, and England. They are truly a (an) _____ family.
   (innovative, covert, transient, heedful, arcane)

2. At _____ school, Mia learned how to prepare the perfect omelet and bake the perfect chocolate mousse cake.
   (itinerant, gluttony, furtive, culinary, unprecedented)

3. It took three buckets of popcorn and two grilled cheese sandwiches to satisfy Meyers's _____ appetite.
   (nomadic, epicurean, fleeting, clandestine, gluttonous)

4. Gunther was a _____ employee, the first person in and the last to leave every day.
   (conscientious, emaciated, innovative, surreptitious, delectable)

5. For most people, liver and onions are not very _____.
   (abstemious, meticulous, furtive, evanescent, palatable)

6. A (An) _____ undercover agent, Roy tried to remain _____ no matter where he went.
   contemporary...stealthy
   clandestine...unprecedented
   surreptitious...covert
   archaic...stealthy
   conspicuous...clandestine

7. It's virtually impossible for a bedazzling _____ like fireworks to be _____.
   relic...sly
   furtive...obtrusive
   inception...stealthy
   antiquity...surreptitious
   spectacle...inconspicuous

8. Be _____ of nutritional advice; even though something might be dreamily _____, it might be a nightmare with regard to dietary value.
   furtive...meticulous
   conscientious...gingerly
   heedful...delectable
   nomadic...innovative
   scrupulous...unprecedented

9. _____ about keeping fat out of every morsel and calorie she ate, Gia began to look _____.
   Volatile...conscientious
   Sly...voracious
   Exacting...epicurean
   Covert...antediluvian
   Vigilant...emaciated

10. _____ when it comes to chocolate, Justin eats this decadent treat _____.
    Obsolete...nomadically
    Circumspect...furtively
    Gluttonous...voraciously
    Surreptitious...fleetingly
    Abstemious...covertly

ONE DOESN'T BELONG

Three of the words in each grouping relate to each other somehow. Cross off the one word that does not belong with the others. For a challenge, write the word that does not belong on the line below, and try your best to define that word. *Note:* Some of the words have been taken from definitions or exercises that appear within the lessons.

1. savory   sly   surreptitious   stealthy

_____ means _____

2. peripatetic   itinerant   fleeting   furtive

_____ means _____

3. unprecedented   unparalleled   novel   antediluvian

_____ means _____

4. delectable   evanescent   culinary   epicurean

_____ means _____

5. painstaking   exacting   meticulous   obsolete

_____ means _____

<table>
<tr><td>

Lesson 26

</td><td>

DO YOU KNOW THESE PEOPLE?

Words Relating to People You Will Meet on the SAT

</td></tr>
</table>

adversary advocate artisan ascetic charlatan demographer hedonist orator pariah raconteur skeptic virtuoso

---

adversary (AD-vuh-ser-ee) *n.* an opponent

To Wanda's frustration, her math teacher seemed more like an **adversary** than a guide through the mysteries of calculus.

Jay and Ken were long-time friends and colleagues, but their disagreement turned them into **adversaries**.

Off the court they are pals, but on the court they play tennis like the fiercest **adversaries**.

advocate (AD-vuh-kut) *n.* a supporter; proponent

As an **advocate** for children, Millie spends her days trying to eradicate all forms of child abuse, neglect, and maltreatment.

My best friend Laura is my eternal **advocate**; she will support me vociferously for the rest of my life.

Are you an **advocate** for increased or decreased spending when it comes to preserving the environment?

artisan (AR-tuh-zun) *n.* a person who is skillful with his or her hands

In Italy, my grandfather worked as an **artisan**, more specifically as a glassblower.

A group of **artisans** was hired to build a charming stone wall around the property.

Every weekend **artisans** display and sell their crafts on the village green.

ascetic (uh-SEH-tik) *n.* a person who refrains from indulging in earthly pleasures

Tiffany lives **ascetically**. Her home is a simple one-room cabin in the woods.

The **ascetic** gave away all his possessions and went to Central America, where he worked as a missionary.

Why would one who claims to be an **ascetic** own five wristwatches and a suitcase full of jewelry?

charlatan (SHAR-luh-tun) *n.* a fraud; a quack or imposter

Charlotte, the new biology teacher, was a **charlatan**. Her college degree was actually in comparative literature.

The book is about a **charlatan**, an uneducated imposter who pretended to be a physician.

Is the minister someone we can trust and believe in, or is he merely a **charlatan**?

demographer (dih-MAH-gruh-fer) *n.* one who studies and engages in the science of vital and social statistics, such as the number of diseases, marriages, births, and deaths of various populations that are under study

As a **demographer**, Demi collected data on the number of births, deaths, and marriages in her suburban community.

Demographers amass and analyze socially vital statistics that characterize a given population.

To illustrate her statistical findings, **demographer** Doris creates charts, bar graphs, and tables.

hedonist (HEE-duh-nist) *n.* a person who lives for pleasure

Michael is too much of a **hedonist** to get a job. He'd rather just play around.

We lived like **hedonists** during our vacation at Club Med. For a week we frolicked on the beach, danced all night, and had nothing but great food and fun.

Her **hedonistic** lifestyle soon grew boring, so Heidi went back to school and to work.

orator (OR-uh-tur) *n.* a skillful public speaker

Martin Luther King's speech, "I Have a Dream," established him as one of the best **orators** of all time.

An acclaimed **orator**, Oliver captivates his audience with his inflection, choice of words, and poignant use of figurative language.

The **orator** received a standing ovation for his outstanding oration. (Try repeating that three times!)

pariah (puh-RIE-uh) *n.* a social outcast

After he painted his house bright orange, Paul became the neighborhood **pariah**. No one on the block wanted anything to do with him.

Hilda is a **pariah**, but she doesn't mind being an outcast because she has poetry to keep her company.

After the scandal, Shoeless Joe became a **pariah**. Expelled from the game, he never played baseball again.

raconteur (ra-kahn-TUR) *n.* a skillful storyteller

Uncle Stephan is our family **raconteur**. He has endless stories to tell about life in the old country.

Rod is a creative **raconteur**. He can make up a fascinating story based on the simplest everyday occurrence.

Mr. Stanley should be more of a teacher and less of a **raconteur**. I'm sick of hearing his stories about the Navy.

skeptic (SKEP-tik) *n.* a person who doubts; one who is dubious or incredulous

Now do you believe in UFOs, or are you still a **skeptic**?

Many **skeptics** still don't accept the conclusions of the Warren Commission.

Mary is **skeptical** about the wisdom of buying on credit, so she pays for everything in cash.

virtuoso (vur-choo-OH-so) *n*. a highly skilled performer, usually a musical performer

Ellen gave a **virtuoso** performance on the court, scoring 60 points and grabbing 24 rebounds.

As a **virtuoso** trumpeter, Danny stands a good chance of getting into the Juilliard School.

Since age six, Sarah has been a **virtuoso** with a violin. At age 12, she started making recordings and performing in concert halls worldwide.

MEMORY TIPS

Use these mnemonics (memory devices) to boost your vocabulary. Make up your own memory clues for words in this lesson that are personally challenging. Add these tips—and your own—to your Vocabulary Notebook. Remember, vocabulary building is key to increasing your score on the verbal SAT.

advocate The Latin root *voc* means voice or call. An **advocate** is one who "calls for" or "voices" the proposal, cause, or point-of-view of another. Consider the root *voc* (or the alternatives *vok* or *vow*) in the following words: e*voc*e, equi*voc*ate, or a*vow*.

raconteur Do you know what it means to *recount* a story? *Recount* is an infinitive verb that means "to tell or to narrate." So you see, a **raconteur** is one who tells stories well.

virtuoso Let the *vi* remind you of *vi*olin. Now imagine a highly-skilled violinist playing classical music. In other words, picture a **virtuoso** performing on stage in your mind's eye.

MATCHING

Match the vocabulary words in Column A with *one or more* of their defining characteristics appearing in Column B.

Column A

1. charlatan
2. raconteur
3. ascetic
4. skeptic
5. orator
6. advocate

Column B

a. a doubter
b. a storyteller
c. a speech maker
d. a self-denying individual
e. an imposter
f. a supporter

SENTENCE COMPLETION

Remember: Answer choices can be the lesson words themselves, or words that appear in definitions or Memory Tips. Select a word form and part of speech that fit correctly within the sentence.

1. On the lacrosse field, your _____ is most likely the one who is swinging a lax stick at you while outstripping you down the field.
   (hedonist, virtuoso, ascetic, orator, adversary)

2. Keeping things simple, some _____ stand behind a podium and use note cards to deliver their speeches. Other public speakers engage in a complex logistical process involving PowerPoint presentations, wireless mouse remotes, and laser pointers—all combined with large white boards on which they write with dry-erase markers.
   (advocates, hedonists, orators, skeptics, pariahs)

3. A born _____, David tells colorful and engaging stories about his days as a scuba-diving instructor and as a dance club disc jockey in Palm Springs, Florida.
   (proponent, raconteur, opponent, artisan, charlatan)

4. A (An) _____ would doubt the existence of extraterrestrial space-craft even if a bunch of green guys with antennas on their heads gave him a joyride through the Milky Way galaxy.
(virtuoso, ascetic, advocate, quack, skeptic)

5. Dressed in a white lab coat and wearing a stethoscope around her neck, Ms. Julep, posing as a cardiac surgeon, was quickly revealed as a (an) _____ when she opened her mouth and spoke nonsense about the blocked artery in my femur bone!
(pariah, adversary, charlatan, raconteur, hedonist)

WORDS IN CONTEXT

Based on the context in which each **bold** word is used, identify the word usage of each sentence as either C (Correct) or I (Incorrect).

1. The masterful **advocate** prepared decadent desserts.

2. Playing three sports well makes one a **virtuoso**.

3. Bruce, a **hedonist** at heart, gives in to his every whim and desire.

4. Living among **charlatans** can make one doubt humankind's authenticity.

5. Silversmiths were widespread **artisans** during America's colonial times.

Lesson 27 | IT JUST DOESN'T MATTER

Words Relating to Things of Little Importance or Value

extraneous frivolous incidental inconsequential irrelevant negligible peripheral petty superficial trifling trivial

---

extraneous (ek-STRAY-nee-us) *adj*. not necessary; not an essential part; not relevant

In your oral report, include only the highlights of your paper. Leave out all **extraneous** matters.

The detective scrutinized the crime scene, taking note of everything, even the most **extraneous** details.

Let's stick to the heart of the matter and put your **extraneous** concerns aside for the moment.

frivolous (FRIH-vuh-lus) *adj*. not having substance, a sense of importance, or seriousness; silly; trivial; trifling

Lenny sued the chef because there was a dead fly in his soup, but the judge threw out the complaint on the grounds that it was **frivolous**.

Forget about looking for a deep meaning in that story. It's totally **frivolous**.

If you ask a silly question, you deserve a **frivolous** response.

incidental (in-suh-DEN-tl) *adj*. less important; minor

An **incidental** benefit of not having your own car is that you walk a lot and get plenty of exercise.

In college, tuition, room, and board make up the bulk of the cost, but there are numerous **incidental** expenses, too.

While studying the scratch on my car, I noticed **incidentally** that I needed air in this tire.

inconsequential (in-kahn-suh-KWEN-shul) *adj.* irrelevant; of no significance; unimportant

The collision produced a huge crash, but the damage to the cars was **inconsequential**.

During the semester, Malcolm failed one quiz, but the impact on his final grade was **inconsequential**.

It's **inconsequential** whether Jean studies math for an hour or for a week. She still earns A's.

irrelevant (ih-REH-luh-vunt) *adj.* not relating to the matter at hand

The fact that Marnie has a cold is **irrelevant** to her cutting classes.

The teacher said that since the essay was awful, the amount of time I spent writing it is **irrelevant** to the grade.

Ron tried to hide the truth with a smokescreen of **irrelevancies**.

negligible (NEH-glih-juh-bul) *adj.* able or likely to be neglected or bypassed due to smallness or lack of importance

Unfortunately, the patient made **negligible** improvement overnight.

Peter refused the job offer because the increase in salary was **negligible**.

Although the tire looked flat, it took only a **negligible** amount of air.

peripheral (puh-RIH-fuh-rul) *adj.* only marginally connected to what is truly important; minor or incidental; at the edge of one's field of vision

The class discussion got bogged down in **peripheral** matters that had nothing to do with the issue of cloning.

What's important to me is the salary. Benefits and everything else are **peripheral**.

Deer have excellent **peripheral** vision. They can see movement in all directions except right behind them.

petty (PEH-tee) *adj.* minor or trivial; not very important or serious; paltry

Igor complained about some **petty** flaws, like lint on the clothing and a wrinkled bedsheet.

Their arguments were about **petty** matters. There was no big issue between them.

The messenger was fired because of the **petty** complaints of his supervisor.

superficial (soo-pur-FIH-shul) *adj.* lacking in depth or importance; on the surface

The paper received a poor grade because I didn't go deeply into Hawthorne's writing. The teacher said I dealt with it only **superficially**.

The wound was **superficial**. It was only skin deep and hardly bled at all.

I hate the **superficial** conversations that I'm forced into at my parents' parties.

trifling (TRY-fling) *adj.* lacking significance; unimportant

In the long run, cutting down one tree may seem **trifling**, but once the precedent is set, the whole forest may be cut down.

"Lying during your college interview is no **trifling** matter," said Mother. "In fact, it could cause you to be rejected."

He called after midnight with some **trifling** news that could easily have waited until morning.

trivial (TRIH-vee-ul) *adj.* unimportant; trifling; ordinary

Because rain is needed badly, the **trivial** amount that fell yesterday is not going to ease the drought.

So much of the class was taken up by **trivialities** that hardly any time was left to discuss important matters.

Gordy is a world-class expert in hockey **trivia**. Ask him anything about pro hockey, and he'll know the answer.

MEMORY TIPS

Use these mnemonics (memory devices) to boost your vocabulary. Make up your own memory clues for words in this lesson that are personally challenging. Add these tips—and your own—to your Vocabulary Notebook. Remember, vocabulary building is key to increasing your score on the verbal SAT.

petty Learn **petty** along with the word *paltry* (unimportant, small). After all, they share three consonants (p, t, y), they start and end with the same letter, and they each have two syllables. **Petty** and *paltry* are an SAT synonym pair. Write them together in your Vocabulary Notebook.

superficial For this word, knowing the prefix *super-* (*above*) is extremely helpful. Superman is *above* other men because of his above-normal strength and power. In addition, notice that the word *surface* can be spelled using the letters found in **superficial**. A **superficial** understanding, then, reaches only the surface level and lacks depth.

MATCHING

Match the vocabulary words in Column A with *one or more* of their defining characteristics appearing in Column B.

Column A

1. superficial
2. trivial
3. extraneous
4. trifling
5. frivolous

Column B

a. unimportant
b. only slightly related
c. shallow; lacking depth
d. insignificant
e. not very serious

SENTENCE COMPLETION

Remember: Answer choices can be the lesson words themselves, or words that appear in definitions or Memory Tips. Select a word form and part of speech that fit correctly within the sentence.

1. Making a trifle is no _____ undertaking; this decadent dessert takes time and involves carefully layering equal parts custard, fresh fruit, and moist cake.
   (extraneous, peripheral, trifling, paltry, negligible)

2. Don't get bent out of shape over another's _____ transgressions; save your fury for something significant and truly troubling.
(petty, consequential, extraneous, relevant, frivolity)

3. Today's women's magazines overly focus on the _____ aspects of a woman's life—like her hair, appearance, and body shape—rather than the internal attributes that make her a unique and dynamic presence in the world.
(petty, irrelevant, trivial, incidental, superficial)

4. _____ expenses (like that pack of gum purchased at checkout or that decaf picked up at the deli) add up and can potentially leave a gap at month's end between expenses and assets.
(Peripheral, Irrelevant, Incidental, Consequential, Paltry)

5. Let's not waste our time with _____ talk about who's dating who and which Hollywood star earns the most money; instead, let's talk about our business priorities for the day.
(negligible, trivial, pettiness, trivia, superficially)

WORDS IN CONTEXT

Based on the context in which each **bold** word is used, identify the word usage of each sentence as either C (Correct) or I (Incorrect).

1. The number of possessions one owns is **trivial** when compared to the number of close family members and friends one has.

2. The association members were disappointed by the **superficiality** of the speaker's topics for discussion.

3. **Frivolous** protests will receive priority status.

4. Despite their **petty** dimes and nickels, the lemonade stand operators were thrilled with their piggy bank stash.

5. Eager to become a world-renowned actor, the young starlet never passed on a stage role, no matter how small or **trifling**.

Lesson 28

LIKE AN OWL

Words Relating to Being Wise and Sharp-Minded

acute astute discerning erudite incisive ingenious judicious
perspicacious prudent sagacious savvy shrewd

---

acute (uh-KYOOT) *adj.* keen-minded; sharp

Because it supposedly improves mental **acuity**, fish is called brain food.

Natalie's **acute** intellect contrasts with the dull minds of her classmates.

Dee had a dull toothache yesterday, but this morning the pain was much more **acute**.

astute (uh-STOOT) *adj.* sharp-minded; very clever

The teacher said, "How **astute** you must be to have found that mistake in the problem. No one has ever noticed it before."

An **astute** lawyer, Jonah wins most of his cases.

As an **astute** reader of poetry, Helen seems always to find meanings hidden between the lines.

discerning (dih-SUR-ning) *adj.* able to judge people and situations clearly

The **discerning** audience easily detected the sarcasm in the comedian's jokes.

As a **discerning** collector, Harry buys only the very best bluegrass recordings on the market.

If you look carefully, you may **discern** a small boat out there in the fog.

erudite (ER-uh-dite) *adj.* wise due to much reading and studying; scholarly

Mr. Major seems like a plain, simple guy, but he is **erudite** and a well-respected scholar of ancient languages.

Morris pretends to be **erudite**, but he's really an airhead.

He attributes his **erudition** to a lifetime of studying and reading good books.

incisive (in-SIE-siv) *adj.* decisive, keen and directly to the point

Brian's **incisive** comments went right to the heart of the matter.

It took many **incisive** minds to figure out the structure of the genome.

No one ever accused Mortimer of having an **incisive** wit. He's as dull as they come.

ingenious (in-JEEN-yus) *adj.* very clever or inventive

The Osprey, an aircraft that lands like a helicopter but flies like a plane, is an **ingenious** invention, but it has had numerous technical problems.

Ingenious it may be, but a digital belt buckle is a pretty useless item.

Claude came up with an **ingenious** alternative to the broken computer: a piece of paper and a pencil.

judicious (joo-DIH-shus) *adj.* showing wisdom in judging people and situations

By keeping to a budget, Marlene makes **judicious** use of her limited income.

Since you get only one guess, think about it **judiciously** beforehand.

Henny chose a college without thinking much about it, but Nora is trying to be more **judicious**.

perspicacious (pur-spuh-KAY-shus) *adj.* using wise judgment; sharp-minded

As a **perspicacious** observer of teenagers, Mr. Krystal knew instantly that Kenny had a problem.

The most **perspicacious** scene in the play is the family dinner. Donna captured a typical dinnertime conversation exactly.

Dana can do a **perspicacious** impersonation of the president's speech, gestures, and facial expressions.

prudent (PROO-dnt) *adj.* careful, cautious, and wise

It is **prudent** not to drive when the roads are covered with ice.

Because he was tired and sleepy, Charles made a **prudent** decision to stop for coffee.

Before agreeing to buy an old house, it would be **prudent** to have the place checked for termites.

sagacious (suh-GAY-shus) *adj.* wise

For a three-year-old, my kid brother says the most **sagacious** things. Unlike me, he may be a budding genius.

Ms. Roth wrote, "This **sagacious** essay is full of impressive insights." From her, that's quite a compliment.

As a **sagacious** observer, Agee was able to recreate just what it was like on a typical summer morning in Knoxville.

savvy (SA-vee) *adj.* smart; informed

The salesman tried to hide the car's defects, but Will was **savvy** enough to find them.

Samantha is **savvy** enough to find her way around San Francisco without a map.

Savvy investors knew better than to put their money in Vince's risky business venture.

shrewd (SHROOD) *adj.* insightful; clever

Dennis was **shrewd** enough not to be deceived by the fast-talking used car salesman.

Marion is a **shrewd** negotiator, always getting the deal she wants but leaving the other side pleased with the outcome.

Jonas scored after faking out the defense with a **shrewd** move up the middle of the field.

MEMORY TIPS

Use these mnemonics (memory devices) to boost your vocabulary. Make up your own memory clues for words in this lesson that are personally challenging. Add these tips—and your own—to your Vocabulary Notebook. Remember, vocabulary building is key to increasing your score on the verbal SAT.

acute As you probably know from your math studies, **acute** angles are those that are less than 90 degrees. In other words, **acute** angles are *sharp*—sharper than obtuse (blunt) angles. So, link *sharp angles* to *sharp-minded* people. Acute can also mean *intense* or *concentrated*, as in "acute pain" or "acute focus."

Note: Obtuse means dim-witted.

incisive Slant rhyme this word with its succinct definition, *decisive*.

judicious Let the *jud* at the beginning of this word make you think of *judge*. I'm sure you agree that a judge ought to be **judicious** (sensible and wise when it comes to "judging" people and their circumstances, for example). Do not confuse **judicious** with *judgmental*; the latter term has to do with criticizing or finding fault.

perspicacious You can build the meaning of this word by knowing the meaning of its prefix and root. The prefix *peri-* means "around." The root *spic* (also *spec* as in *spectator* or *inspect*) has to do with "looking or seeing." So, **perspicacious** has to do with "looking and seeing all around." If one is **perspicacious**, then one is also perceptive—able to clearly see through and around.

MATCHING

Match the vocabulary words in Column A with *one or more* of their defining characteristics appearing in Column B.

Column A	Column B
1. sagacious	a. showing good judgment
2. prudent	b. sharp, intense
3. perspicacious	c. like a sage or wise elder
4. acute	d. perceptive
5. ingenious	e. imaginative and clever

SENTENCE COMPLETION

Remember: Answer choices can be the lesson words themselves, or words that appear in definitions or Memory Tips. Select a word form and part of speech that fit correctly within the sentence.

1. _____ stomach discomfort can sometimes be lessened by drinking chamomile tea and resting in a quiet, dark room.
   (Acute, Savvy, Judicious, Shrewd, Perspicacious)

2. A (An) _____ shopper, Janna knows how to take advantage of every red-line sale, clearance event, and double-coupon promotion.
   (discerningly, shrewd, acuity, erudite, ingenious)

3. Hank had made a name for himself as reckless and wayward—but now, after turning over a new leaf, he is the epitome of _____ and selectivity.
   (savvy, sagacity, prudence, erudition, obtuseness)

4. As a writer and researcher who can get her hands on almost any information she needs, including original documents, Mariella is far beyond resourceful, she is _____.
   (ingenious, judicious, erudite, acute, prudent)

5. Making the public library her second home, Justine is more than a casual bookworm; she is a (an) _____ young lady.
   (shrewd, perspicacious, acumen, prudent, erudite)

WORDS IN CONTEXT

Based on the context in which each **bold** word is used, identify the word usage of each sentence as either C (Correct) or I (Incorrect).

1. Building a new kind of doghouse might be the undertaking of an **ingenious** individual.

2. **Prudent** investing involves the random selection of stocks and mutual funds.

3. "Very **sagacious**, Myrtle. You knew just what the Grubers were thinking."

4. An **incisive** mentality understands issues and circumstances on a surface level.

5. Listening attentively to both sides of the dispute and taking into consideration all relevant details, Ella handled the debacle **judiciously**.

TRICKY TWINS AND TRIPLETS
Words That Sound and/or Look Alike, But Have Different Meanings

acrid/arid aesthetic/ascetic/atheistic ambiguous/ambivalent coalesce/convalesce delusion/allusion/illusion

---

acrid (A-crud) *adj.* bitter, harsh

Acrid exhaust fumes from the traffic inside the tunnel made him cough.

The comedian's **acrid** humor rubbed salt into many wounds.

The **acrid** smell inside the room made me gag.

arid (A-rid) *adj.* dry, lacking water

On one side of the island it rains all the time; the other side is totally **arid**.

The arroyo once had running water in it, but now is **arid**.

Arid air inside the plane dries my skin.

aesthetic (es-THEH-tik) *adj.* having to do with artistic beauty

To build a house that ugly shows a lack of **aesthetic** taste.

Bertha gets her sense of **aesthetics** from her mother, who is a successful artist and designer.

There is something **aesthetically** wrong with that painting. It pushes you away instead of drawing you in.

ascetic (uh-SEH-tik) (from Lesson 26) *n.* a person who refrains from indulging in earthly pleasures

Tiffany lives like an **ascetic**. Her home is a simple one-room cabin in the woods.

The **ascetic** gave away all his possessions and went to Central America, where he worked as a missionary.

Why would one who claims to be an **ascetic** own five wristwatches and a suitcase full of jewelry?

atheistic (ay-thee-IS-tik) *adj.* without a belief in any god

Although James was raised as a strict Catholic, he became an **atheist** in college.

Although they don't believe in God, **atheists** can still experience spirituality.

Henry tried to convince his **atheistic** brother that God exists.

ambiguous (am-BIH-gyuh-wus) *adj.* hard to understand; unclear; open to more than one interpretation

Because Hester's answer was totally **ambiguous**, I don't know whether she agrees or disagrees.

By leaving the passage **ambiguous**, the author wants the reader to decide what it means.

People who prefer definite answers are often uncomfortable with **ambiguity**.

ambivalent (am-BIH-vuh-lunt) *adj.* having conflicting feelings or opinions about something; unsure

Rose feels **ambivalent** about the weekend in Vermont. She wants to go, but she also wants to stay at home.

Ambivalence paralyzes Penny; she can't make up her mind about anything.

If you expect to win the argument, be confident that you are right. **Ambivalence** will be taken as a sign of weakness.

coalesce (koe-uh-LES) *vb.* to have different opinions join together; fuse; converge

By the end of the meeting, the various viewpoints somehow **coalesced** into a coherent policy.

The legislators **coalesced** behind Senator Cooke and elected her unanimously.

Gravity caused billions of atoms to **coalesce** into a single lump of rock.

convalesce (kahn-vuh-LES) *vb*. to recover from an illness

After her hip surgery, Grandma **convalesced** at home instead of in the hospital.

A **convalescence** of two months kept Joe from his job.

While **convalescing** from a leg wound, Lt. Henry fell in love with his nurse.

delusion (dih-LOO-zhun) *n*. a false opinion or belief

To expect to get into Yale with an 880 SAT score is nothing but a **delusion**.

"It might be self-**delusion** or wishful thinking, but I think that Barry has fallen in love with me," said Brenda.

The story tells of a lowly clerk who has **deluded** himself into thinking he's the king of Spain.

allusion (uh-LOO-zhun) *n*. an indirect reference, often to a character or theme found in some work of literature

The book is hard to read unless you understand the author's **allusions** to Greek and Roman mythology.

Carla interpreted the poet's reference to "hound dog" as an **allusion** to Elvis.

It's as though Mr. Hargrove is living in the past. He always **alludes** to the 1960s when he wants to make a point.

illusion (ih-LOO-zhun) *n*. something unreal that gives the appearance of being real; a misconception

David Blaine, the street magician, creates the spellbinding **illusion** of levitating six inches off the ground.

Although he mainly draws stick figures, Morris harbors the **illusion** that he is a great artist.

My favorite magic trick is the **illusion** of turning a cup of coffee into a cup full of shiny pennies.

MEMORY TIPS

Use these mnemonics (memory devices) to boost your vocabulary. Make up your own memory clues for words in this lesson that are personally challenging. Add these tips—and your own—to your Vocabulary Notebook.

ambiguous, ambivalent As a prefix, *ambi-* means *both*. If you didn't know this prefix, then you might have known *bi-*, meaning *two*. In either case, the idea of *both* or *two* is behind the meanings of these vocabulary words. To review, the first listed means "having two (or more) meanings"; the second, "having two conflicting feelings about something or someone." Ambidexterous means being able to use your left and right hands skillfully.

arid Have you heard of the antiperspirant Arrid? Well, the commercials tell us that Arrid keeps you "extra *dry*." Who says television isn't educational?

MATCHING

Match the vocabulary words in Column A with *one or more* of their defining characteristics appearing in Column B.

Column A	Column B
1. illusion	a. denying oneself pleasure
2. convalesce	b. harsh, biting
3. allusion	c. a reference
4. ascetic	d. a magic trick
5. acrid	e. to get well again

SENTENCE COMPLETION

Remember: Answer choices can be the lesson words themselves, or words that appear in definitions or Memory Tips. Select a word form and part of speech that fit correctly within the sentence.

1. _____ perspectives make for an enlightening debate; seeing eye-to-eye can be both boring and blinding.
   (Ambivalent, Coalescent, Divergent, Acrid, Ascetic)

2. People with dry coughs sometimes put humidifiers in their bedrooms to counteract the _____ inside air.
   (atheistic, acrid, convalescing, delusional, arid)

3. The action-adventure author included several _____ to Hercules in an effort to describe the protagonist's great physical strength.
   (illusions, delusions, aesthetics, ambiguities, allusions)

4. Alyssa needed several weeks to fully _____ from her caesarean section after delivering her beautiful twin boys.
   (convalesce, ambiguous, delusion, ambidextrous, coalesce)

5. When Jamie speaks, he is a crystal-clear open book, but his facial expressions are so _____ that even his fiancée has difficulty in discerning whether he is pleased or disgruntled.
   (coalescent, acrid, ambiguous, illusionary, arid)

WORDS IN CONTEXT

Based on the context in which each **bold** word is used, identify the word usage of each sentence as either C (Correct) or I (Incorrect).

1. As an **ascetic**, Edgar prefers to live in a dry climate.

2. The **delusions** that Mario the Great Magician performed on stage played with Sabrina's mind for days after the show.

3. When opinions **coalesce**, conflicts eventually subside.

4. People who regularly go to museums and art galleries have strong **aesthetic** interests.

5. **Acrid** rumors can sometimes hurt an individual as much as physical injury.

MORE TRICKY TWINS AND TRIPLETS

imprudent/impudent indigenous/indigent/indignant
intimate/intimidate obscure/obtuse ponderable/ponderous

---

imprudent (im-PROO-dnt) *adj.* careless; rash

Quitting her job in a moment of anger proved to be **imprudent**; Lindsay would not be able to save enough money to attend her own senior prom.

Jogging at night without wearing reflective clothing is **imprudent**.

It is **imprudent** to wait until the last minute to register for classes. All the good classes fill up quickly.

impudent (IM-pyuh-dunt) *adj.* rude; disrespectful

Answering my father in an **impudent** manner guaranteed that I would lose car privileges for at least a week.

The teacher decided she had had enough of the class's **impudent** behavior and gave them all detention.

The group of kids sitting in the back of the movie theater was so loud and **impudent** that the usher made them leave.

indigenous (in-DIH-juh-nus) *adj.* native; originating in a specific country or region

Eucalyptus trees grow all over the world, but they are **indigenous** to Australia.

Indigenous people in the United States are called Native Americans.

Pineapples are **indigenous** to Hawaii.

indigent (IN-dih-junt) *adj.* poor; impoverished; needy

Angela's Ashes is the story of an **indigent** family living hand-to-mouth in the slums of Limerick, Ireland.

As a lawyer for the Legal Aid Society, Martin represents **indigent** clients in court.

The movie is about a middle-class girl who winds up **indigent** on the streets of Chicago.

indignant (in-DIG-nunt) *adj*. angry; resentful

Mr. Jason became **indignant** when Jake interrupted the performance by asking to go to the bathroom.

Billy's insulting and crude remarks left Mama upset and **indignant**.

What makes me most **indignant** is someone cutting in line ahead of me.

intimate (IN-tuh-mate) *vb*. to suggest; to hint at

My college advisor **intimated** that if I kept my grades up I might qualify for a scholarship.

When Jennifer told Mike that he looked slim, Mike replied, "Are you **intimating** that I used to look fat?"

The principal **intimated** that school might be closed if heavy snow is predicted.

intimidate (in-TIM-i-date) *vb*. to frighten; to coerce into action

At 6 feet 4 inches tall and 240 pounds, Ben easily **intimidates** little kids just by glaring at them.

Now that she has mastered kung fu, Cherri is no longer **intimidated** when she crosses the campus alone at night.

Marcy is **intimidated** by standardized tests, but she is learning to deal with her fears.

obscure (ahb-SKYOOR) *adj*. hard to understand; abstract

The point of the story is a little **obscure**, but the characters are crystal clear.

Maria found an allusion to an **obscure** monk in 14th-century Italy who invented what we now call a pencil.

Tom started as an **obscure** actor in the provinces, but now he's world famous.

obtuse (ahb-TOOS) *adj*. stupid; not clear or precise

Are you being deliberately **obtuse** or are you just naturally stupid?

I hate to appear **obtuse**, but I just don't understand quadratic equations.

Even after remarking about my out-of-state license plates, the officer still asked **obtuse** questions about whether I was a resident of this state.

ponderable (PAHN-duh-ruh-bul) *adj*. important enough to require a lot of thought

Whether to skip classes to take a driving test is an easy question for some people, but for Cynthia it's a **ponderable** dilemma.

It's a **ponderable** issue whether to break up with Keith before the prom or after the prom.

Dad said, "I don't have time for a **ponderable** question on the meaning of life just now. Let's discuss it over dinner, okay?"

ponderous (PAHN-duh-rus) *adj*. very heavy or bulky; dull or lifeless

Willa Cather's style of writing is **ponderous** to read. I prefer something more energetic and lively.

It's hard to believe how the filmmaker turned an exciting adventure story into a dark, **ponderous** tale of jealousy and betrayal.

It's a slow, **ponderous** novel about a poor fisherman and his net. It was supposed to be deep, but the meaning escaped me.

MEMORY TIPS

Use these mnemonics (memory devices) to boost your vocabulary. Make up your own memory clues for words in this lesson that are challenging for you. Add these tips—and your own—to your Vocabulary Notebook.

indigent This clue will not help you distinguish **indigent** from its tricky triplets, yet this clue will help you remember this word on its own. Let the *indi* at the beginning remind you of India, which is a Third World country that suffers from substantial poverty. Again, be alert to words that might cause confusion, since they look or sound similar to this word. In other words, remember the different meanings of indigent, indigenous, and indignant.

intimate When you say this word aloud for practice, add an "h" sound to the beginning to get *(h)intimate*. If you say the word so many times in that way, it should stick. So from now on, think *(h)intimate*.

obtuse Chances are you know that **obtuse** angles are greater than 90 degrees, right? So, what kind of "point" is formed by an obtuse angle? A blunt one. That's right, **obtuse** means *blunt*, as in blunt-minded, not-so-sharp, or simply stupid. Remember not to confuse this word with *obscure*.

MATCHING

Match the vocabulary words in Column A with *one or more* of their defining characteristics appearing in Column B.

Column A	Column B
1. indigenous	a. angry
2. obscure	b. bulky to carry
3. indignant	c. hard to understand
4. ponderous	d. hint at
5. ponderable	e. requiring a lot of thought
6. intimate	f. native
7. intimidate	g. to frighten

SENTENCE COMPLETION

Remember: *Answer choices can be the lesson words themselves, or words that appear in definitions or Memory Tips. Select a word form and part of speech that fit correctly within the sentence.*

1. You comment that I seem relaxed today. Are you _____ that I am usually uptight?
   (pondering, indigenous, imprudent, intimating, intimidating)

2. Sadly, it can be very difficult for children from _____ households to thrive and excel in school; without a nutritious breakfast, warm and properly-fitting clothing, and school supplies, children could have a hard time reaching their personal best.
(indigent, ponderous, impudent, indigenous, indignant)

3. Discouragingly, your semester grades point to a (an) _____ mind, but what's really holding you back from better grades are your _____ study habits; waiting until the night before to study for a major social studies test, for example, is not very conscientious.
(indigent...ponderable, obtuse...imprudent, intimidated...obscure, indigenous...ponderous, impudent...obtuse)

4. Although Jake thought that mangoes came exclusively from Brazil, he soon discovered that these luscious fruits are also _____ to Costa Rica.
(indigenous, ponderous, intimating, obtuse, impoverished)

5. It is one thing to move around wicker or bamboo furniture; it's quite another endeavor to resituate several _____ pieces such as a mahogany china closet, seven-foot-long sofa table, and dining room buffet.
(indigent, impudent, ponderable, indignant, ponderous)

WORDS IN CONTEXT

Based on the context in which each **bold** word is used, identify the word usage of each sentence as either C (Correct) or I (Incorrect).

1. Entering the boxing ring, Eric felt **intimidated** by his fierce-looking opponent.

2. Jim is someone who likes things cut-and-dry, to the point. He is certainly not comfortable with **obscurities**.

3. Bruce became **indigent** upon learning that his classmate stole his research project idea.

4. To Helen, Jasmine is a puzzling character. In fact, Jas is an outright **obtuse** individual.

5. Greek philosophers like Aristotle and Sophocles present some of the most **ponderable** ideas about human life.

Review Exercises / Lessons 26–30

VOCABULARY-IN-CONTEXT PARAGRAPH

The paragraph below primarily features words that appear in vocabulary lessons 26–30. For added reinforcement, additional vocabulary words from other lessons may appear in the paragraph. In those cases, the lesson number in which those words appear is indicated within parentheses. In light of the context, the words' meanings should be clear. If you are uncertain about particular meanings, however, take a moment to review the word's definition and illustrative sentences, as provided within the referenced lessons.

Lessons 26–30: The Wise Hedonist

No longer satiated with *lavish* luxuries such as European vacations, pricey home furnishings, and high-end dining, the *sagacious hedonist* decided to indulge in *aesthetic* pleasures instead. To her delight, she found satisfaction in things that she would otherwise have regarded as *inconsequential*. Now, intoxicatingly, peace and contentment *coalesced* as she would give herself to the *euphonious* (Lesson 18), stirring voice of *virtuoso* Andrea Botticelli, take a brisk autumn walk, or experiment— to her family's amusement—with becoming a culinary *artisan*. Firmly, she made the decision to supplant all forms of *indignation* in her midst with either *ponderable* ideals or *judicious* sentiments. Ultimately, the wise hedonist possessed no *ambiguity* about life's greatest gifts and how to live among them.

NAME THAT CLUSTER

To the left of the groups of words, put the Roman numeral that corresponds with these theme (or cluster) titles:

Words Relating to . . .

I. People You Will Meet on the SAT
II. Tricky Twins and Triplets (Words Often Confused)
III. Things of Little Importance or Value

IV. Being Wise and Sharp-Minded

Cluster Title _____	1. shrewd, acute, perspicacious, sagacious, astute
Cluster Title _____	2. virtuoso, skeptic, artisan, hedonist, charlatan
Cluster Title _____	3. petty, trifling, peripheral, negligible, trivial
Cluster Title _____	4. indignant, indigenous, ponderable, ponderous, obtuse, obscure

---

SENTENCE COMPLETION

Note: On the new SAT (March 2016 and forward), multiple-choice sentence completion questions have been eliminated. However, sentence completion questions remain in this book as a vocabulary-strengthening exercise. Make flashcards for the words that are unknown or unfamiliar to you.

Read each sentence carefully. Then, from the five vocabulary words given in parentheses, circle the word that *best* completes each of the sentences below.

1. The tropical island's _____ fruits include papaya and mango. Both are readily available and picked fresh daily from the island's bountiful fruit trees.
(obscure, artisan, indigenous, peripheral, paltry)

2. The _____ sculpted beautiful bowls, pitchers, and vases from clay. The clay took on new life in his hands.
(virtuoso, charlatan, diva, artisan, ascetic)

3. Your threats do not _____ me, but your boxing gloves do.
(adversary, intimate, indignant, obscure, intimidate)

4. No experiment could convince the _____ that the scientist had discovered a new function of the living cell.
(skeptic, intimate, indigent, astute, diva, charlatan)

5. _____ activities include thumb-wrestling and bubble-blowing.
(Peripheral, Gluttonous, Artisan, Frivolous, Ponderous)

6. Toting a cello and masquerading as a (an) _____, the unusual man had no musical talent whatsoever; he was a (an) _____.
pariah...trifling
virtuoso...charlatan
orator...raconteur
illusion...ambiguity
atheist...aesthete

7. Todd's _____ mind allowed him to easily discern the difference between consequential matters and _____ issues.
ascetic...adversarial
oratory...trifling
extraneous...incidental
incisive...petty
negligible...paltry

8. As his statements became more _____, what he was trying to tell us became more _____.
ambiguous...obscure
frivolous...indigenous
irrelevant...aesthetic
petty...erudite
sagacious...ambivalent

9. The furniture mover became increasingly _____ when, time after time, he simply could not find a way to get the _____ chest of drawers up the steps and around the tight corner leading to the bedroom.
ambivalent...aesthetic
paltry...acute
indigenous...intimidating
indignant...ponderous
impudent...trifling

10. Open-minded Hank is far from being a (an) _____; in fact, he considers all theories, no matter how far-fetched, _____, and therefore worthy of his time and consideration.
ascetic...illusionary
orator...incidental
advocate...hedonistic
intimidator...imprudent
skeptic...ponderable

11. Donna gives _____ instructions during her yoga class to pre-
    clude her students from suffering injuries and having to sustain
    periods of _____.
    trifling...perspicacity
    prudent...convalescence
    indignant...indigence
    oratory...asceticism
    ambivalent...superficiality

12. Using hot and vibrant colors, the Mexican _____ painted a
    large clay wall plaque, shaped like the sun.
    (hedonist, illusionist, ascetic, atheist, artisan)

ONE DOESN'T BELONG

Three of the words in each grouping relate to each other somehow.
Cross off the one word that does not belong with the others. For a challenge, write the word that does not belong on the line below, and try
your best to define that word. *Note:* Some of the words have been taken
from definitions or exercises that appear within the lessons.

1. paltry   petty   inconsequential   sagacious

   _____ means _____

2. perspicacious   peripheral   prudent   discerning

   _____ means _____

3. virtuoso   artisan   pariah   raconteur

   _____ means _____

abridge accessible antidote aspire autonomous bolster
candor cynical fastidious gratify

abridge (uh-BRIDJ) *vb.* shorten

This is the **abridged** version of *David Copperfield*. It contains only 200 pages instead of the original 800.

The school day was **abridged** because teachers were holding parent conferences in the afternoon.

In order to show the film within the two-hour time slot, it was **abridged**.

accessible (ik-SEH-suh-bul) *adj.* available; ready for use

Ramps make the restaurant **accessible** to wheelchair-bound patrons.

The Hubble telescope has given astronomers **access** to galaxies never seen before.

Mrs. Kramer is **accessible** to students who need extra help after school.

antidote (AN-tih-dote) *n.* something that relieves or prevents; a remedy that counteracts the effects of poison

Advil is an effective **antidote** for the pain of a torn ligament.

Acupuncture has been used for centuries as an **antidote** against whatever ails you.

If an **antidote** for world hunger could be found, Earth would be a more congenial place.

aspire (uh-SPIRE) *vb.* to work toward or to have a goal

Vickie **aspires** to be a prima ballerina some day. To dance on the stage is her dream.

Lem **aspired** to go to college out of town, but he couldn't afford anything but the local community college.

If you **aspire** to play hockey for the school, you'd better practice your skating.

autonomous (aw-TAH-nuh-mus) *adj.* independent

Maggie blossomed once she left home and became **autonomous**.

"With **autonomy** comes responsibility," said the dean.

While others worked on the research in teams, Eddie did the experiments **autonomously**.

bolster (BOLE–stur) *vb.* to support; to strengthen

Pumping iron has **bolstered** Laura's confidence and self-esteem.

A healthy diet **bolsters** your body's resistance to disease.

One's chances of getting into college can be **bolstered** by writing an effective application essay.

candor (KAN-dur) *n.* honesty, sincerity; speaking or conducting oneself with a measure of earnestness

"I want complete **candor** from you," said Ms. Flynn. "Is this your own work or is it someone else's?"

Politicians rarely speak with total **candor** because they don't want to offend anyone by revealing how they actually feel about controversial issues.

I know she expects **candor** from me, but if I told her the truth she'd be devastated.

cynical (SIH-nih-kul) *adj.* believing that all others are motivated by self-interest

As a basically **cynical** person, Holden distrusts everyone he meets.

Jo, a **cynic** to the core, thinks everyone is up to no good.

I'm **cynical** about the overnight change in Louis' personality. He must have an ulterior motive for changing from a thug to a saint.

fastidious (fa-STIH-dee-us) *adj.* very attentive to detail; fussy; meticulous

Martha is a **fastidious** homemaker; everything is neat and clean at her house.

A **fastidious** dresser, Annette looks as though she's just stepped out of a fashion magazine.

Juan's homework is **fastidiously** prepared. He takes the time to make it perfect in every way.

gratify (GRA-tuh-fie) *vb.* to please or indulge

Julia **gratifies** her sweet tooth with chocolate Kisses and jelly beans.

I'm pleased that my kid brother gets good grades. It's **gratifying** to see him learning from my mistakes.

The coach, who worked hard to develop his players' skills, was **gratified** by their progress.

MEMORY TIPS

Use these mnemonics (memory devices) to boost your vocabulary. Make up your own memory clues for words in this lesson that are challenging for you. Add these tips—and your own—to your Vocabulary Notebook.

abridge Think about how a *bridge* shortens the travel distance between two points.

autonomous As a prefix, *auto-* means *self*. This word really means *self-rule*. Self-rule is essentially independence. Consider these words that contain the prefix *auto-*: automated, automaton, autoimmune, autocrat, automobile. See how *self* plays a role in the meaning of each of these words.

fastidious Let the *f* and *s* sounds at the beginning of this word remind you of *fussy*. Also, remember this vocabulary word's SAT-level synonym, *meticulous*. Like **fastidious**, *meticulous* is an adjective that ends in *-ous* and has four syllables.

MATCHING

Match the vocabulary words in Column A with *one or more* of their defining characteristics appearing in Column B.

Column A	Column B
1. bolster	a. frankness; forthrightness
2. autonomous	b. to have a goal
3. accessible	c. available for use
4. candor	d. to shorten
5. abridge	e. something that counteracts illness
6. aspire	f. dependent on self
7. fastidious	g. to support
8. gratify	h. pessimistic about people's motives
9. cynical	i. to please
10. antidote	j. fussy

SENTENCE COMPLETION

Remember: Answer choices can be the lesson words themselves, or words that appear in definitions or Memory Tips. Select a word form and part of speech that fit correctly within the sentence.

1. Feeling more and more _____, Niki embraced the vibrant and strong-winged butterfly as her symbol of newfound independence.
   (bolstered, abridged, autonomous, cynical, accessible)

2. Forget chamomile tea and bubble baths—a dark fudge brownie is a reliable _____ for a stressful day, since chocolate releases the body's feel-good endorphins and allays anxiety.
   (aspiration, antidote, candor, bolster, fastidious)

3. To _____ his performance on the college-entrance exams, Paul speaks to himself. His self-edifying internal dialogue goes something like this: "I can do it. I've got what it takes. I will sit here and show them all that I know. I am as bright as they come."
   (aspire, meticulous, autonomy, abridge, bolster)

4. If you _____ your column from a thousand words to 750, you will _____ your editor, who favors succinct writing, and you will increase your chances of being assigned another column in the future.
   (bolster...candor, abridge...gratify, aspire...antidote, gratify...automate, access...fastidious)

5. Whereas Lucille is a verbal illusionist—her words shrouded in smoke and shadowy swirls—Lucinda's speech is refreshingly clear, since she speaks with pure _____.
   (autonomy, accessibility, candor, cynicism, aspiration)

WORDS IN CONTEXT

Based on the context in which each **bold** word is used, identify the word usage as either C (Correct) or I (Incorrect).

1. As her usual **cynical** self, Andrea appreciated the good qualities in all people.

2. The magazine editor asked the writer to **abridge** her column since there wasn't enough space to print the entire piece.

3. Yolanda's compliments certainly **bolstered** Drew's struggling ego.

4. The look and fragrance of aromatherapy candles **gratify** my frazzled senses.

5. Do you **aspire** after a long workout at the gym?

hamper hardy homogeneous integrity intrepid linger lofty mock nurture opportunist proximity

---

hamper (HAM-pur) *vb.* to hinder; to prevent something from happening

Phone calls **hampered** Roger's effort to finish his lab report.

A sore knee **hampered** Jim's rigorous training.

I could not hear what Manuela said. Static **hampered** our phone conversation.

hardy (HAR-dee) *adj.* healthy and strong; robust

These plants are **hardy**. They'll grow anywhere.

Anyone who can down nine meatballs, a huge bowl of fusilli, and a whole cantaloupe for lunch has to have a **hardy** digestive tract.

The girls are **hardy** enough to withstand a few rain showers during the hike.

homogeneous (hoe-muh-JEE-nee-us) *adj.* of the same kind; alike; uniform

Of all the states, Utah has the most **homogeneous** population. More than 70 percent of the people are Mormon.

Homogeneous grouping of students according to their ability has long been a sticky issue in public education.

The houses on my block are **homogeneous**. You can hardly tell them apart.

integrity (in-TEH-gruh-tee) *n.* holding firmly to values, such as honesty; completeness

They called him a man of **integrity** only because no one realized that he was a crook.

The **integrity** of the building was damaged by the earth tremors.

Wallace has no **integrity**. He'll do anything to beat the competition, even break the law if necessary.

intrepid (in-TREH-pud) *adj.* fearless; brave

Intrepidly, Columbus sailed west, urging his men to show courage, too.

An **intrepid** stuntman, Steve bravely hurled himself into the ocean far below.

In his youth Matthew was **intrepid**, but as he aged, his innate courage began to falter.

linger (LING-gur) *vb.* to hang around; to stay

Maribeth **lingered** after class to talk with the teacher in private.

The smell of Marlene's perfume **lingered** in the room long after she had left.

Daylight **lingers** in the sky past nine o'clock on summer evenings.

lofty (LAHF-tee) *adj.* very high; towering; grand or noble

Ethan has **lofty** goals. In fact, he expects to be president someday.

Chris' goal is less **lofty**. She hopes to be a schoolteacher.

Marylou dreams **lofty** dreams. I hope she won't be disappointed when reality brings her back to earth.

mock (MAHK) *vb.* to make fun of; to imitate

When Nathan made fun of Sandy, the teacher let him have it: "**Mock** anyone again, Nathan, and your presence in this class is history!"

Mickey's satirical letter to the editor **mocked** the silly new rules in the cafeteria.

Mockingbirds get their name from their ability to imitate, or **mock**, the songs of other birds.

nurture (NUR-chur) *vb.* to care for, to nourish

The Wild Child is the true story of a boy lost in the woods and **nurtured** by wolves until he was about 12 years old.

Since childhood, Julia has **nurtured** the idea of becoming a movie star.

In spite of being **nurtured** in a tolerant environment, Kyle became a bigot.

opportunist (ah-pur-TOO-nist) *n.* a person who seeks self-gain, even at the expense of others, without regard to values or moral principles

Always an **opportunist**, Mac saw Ellen's breakup as a chance to ask her out.

The community thinks the developer is an **opportunist**, more interested in making a dollar than preserving the beauty of the town.

Richie's ambition has made him an **opportunist**. To get ahead he'll do anything, even break the law and hurt others.

proximity (prahk-SIH-muh-tee) *n.* nearness in time, location, relation

Because our house is in **proximity** to the airport, I hear planes all day long.

Ally and Julie arranged to get lockers in **proximity** to each other so they could talk between classes.

Please bring me the carton that's standing in **proximity** to the computer station.

MEMORY TIPS

Use these mnemonics (memory devices) to boost your vocabularly. Make up your own memory clues for words in this lesson that are challenging for you. Add these tips—and your own—to your Vocabulary Notebook.

intrepid Think of the World War II aircraft carrier the USS *Intrepid*, which won fame in numerous Pacific campaigns and battles. She became known as "the Fighting I" after surviving multiple conventional and kamikaze attacks.

lofty Do you know what a *loft* is? (Answer: An upper story of a warehouse, balcony, or attic.) Well then, a loft is an area that is *up high*. Link this information (information that you already might have known) to the meaning of the adjective, **lofty**.

proximity Link this word to one you already know: a<u>proxim</u>ately. *Approximately* means *nearly*, which is related to one meaning of **proximity**, *nearness*. Notice how these words share the letters *proxim*. Again, link something you are familiar with to something new, and you will remember the new vocabulary word more readily. Underline <u>proxim</u> when you write <u>proxim</u>ity in your Vocabulary Notebook.

MATCHING

Match the vocabulary words in Column A with *one or more* of their defining characteristics appearing in Column B.

Column A	Column B
1. hamper	a. healthy
2. intrepid	b. having no fear
3. proximity	c. seeker of self-gain
4. nurture	d. high, high up
5. opportunist	e. to hang around
6. linger	f. alike
7. hardy	g. closeness
8. integrity	h. sincerity
9. lofty	i. to care for
10. mock	j. to ridicule
11. homogeneous	k. impede

SENTENCE COMPLETION

Remember: Answer choices can be the lesson words themselves, or words that appear in definitions or Memory Tips. Select a word form and part of speech that fit correctly within the sentence.

1. If they are in poor taste, even seemingly benign knock-knock jokes can _____ people, their values, and customs.
(mock, nurture, hamper, linger, intrepid)

2. Living in close _____ to one's neighbors can be cozy and comforting, but living on top of one another can be suffocating.
(integrity, homogeneity, opportunism, loft, proximity)

3. A diehard _____, Chuck has no qualms about _____ someone else's progress and honest efforts in order to push himself ahead of the competition.
(nurturer...lingering, hamper...proximity, opportunist...hampering, mocker...intrepidly, lofty...hardy)

4. A (An) _____ breakfast that includes sprouted grain bread and two eggs allows me to face my day _____, no matter what challenges, obstacles, or arduous undertakings the day presents.
(homogeneous...loftily, opportunistic...integrity, nurturing...approximately, hardy...intrepidly, mocking...lingeringly)

5. A bundle of energy, goal-oriented Juanita is not one to _____ around; instead, her body moves purposefully and vigorously throughout the day as she moves from one task or project to the next.
(mock, nurture, hamper, linger, lofty)

WORDS IN CONTEXT

Based on the context in which each **bold** word is used, identify the word usage of each sentence as either C (Correct) or I (Incorrect).

1. An animal cell and a plant cell are **homogeneous.**

2. A daredevil at heart, Gus nicknamed himself "The **Intrepid** One."

3. Jessie decided that Ben's not returning her phone calls might **hamper** their relationship.

4. Phil was **mocked** by his soccer teammates for being the season's most frequent goal-scorer.

5. **Lingering** in bed in the morning was not Dana's style. Instead, she was up and on the go: on her treadmill for 30 minutes, then e-mailing her coworkers.

HOTTEST OF THE HOT WORDS

Letters Q to Z

querulous recount rigor saturate scrutinize surpass
tentative thrive tranquility uniformity vilify whimsical

---

querulous (KWER-yuh-lus) *adj.* whining; complaining

The baby gets **querulous** when she's tired. Her crankiness means she needs a nap.

Always whining and complaining **querulously**, Zeena made life miserable for Ethan.

Every time the teacher gives homework, the class becomes **querulous**. I've never seen such complainers.

recount (rih-KOWNT) *vb.* to tell a story

Let me **recount** what happened in the park on Sunday afternoon. It's a good story.

Grandpa loves to **recount** tales of his carefree youth.

The attorney asked the witness to **recount** what he saw on the evening of May 3rd.

rigor (RIH-gur) *n.* harshness; severity; strict adherence to standards

Because the course lacks **rigor**, Holly is bored. She'd much prefer a more challenging class.

There's no more **rigorous** event than the Iron Man triathlon—swimming two miles, biking 100 miles, and then running a marathon.

To endure the **rigors** of winter at the South Pole, one needs perseverance and a bit of masochism.

saturate (SA-chuh-rate) *vb.* to wet or soak completely; to totally fill up

Billy has **saturated** the school with posters for the dance. You can't go anywhere in the building without seeing one.

The web site is **saturated** with ads—so many, in fact, that they interfere with the purpose of the site.

The field is **saturated**. It's too wet to play on—game postponed.

scrutinize (SKROO-tuh-nize) *vb.* to read or look at very closely and carefully

Gus **scrutinized** the sports section for the scores of yesterday's high school football games, but he couldn't find them, no matter how hard he looked.

As we entered the stadium, the ticket takers **scrutinized** our faces as though they were searching for someone in particular.

With a red pen in hand, Mr. Harvey **scrutinizes** our writing, looking for mistakes in grammar and usage.

surpass (sur-PAS) *vb.* to be better than; to excel

The suspense in the movie **surpassed** my expectations. I had no idea that a documentary could be so riveting.

Dad told me that I had long ago **surpassed** him as an athlete and scholar.

Mike ran the marathon not to win the race, but to **surpass** last year's time.

tentative (TEN-tuh-tiv) *adj.* hesitant; not definite

Ice-skating is **tentatively** planned for Saturday. If the weather stays cold, we'll go; if it warms up, we'll do something else.

Rose, who is afraid of heights, feels **tentative** about her rock-climbing date with Charles. In fact, the jitters have started.

There's a **tentative** agreement to settle the strike, but the workers must vote first.

thrive (THRIVE) *vb.* to grow strong; to flourish

Redwoods **thrive** along the California coast.

Little children **thrive** emotionally with lots of praise and love.

Mr. Kroc built a hamburger stand into a **thriving** business called McDonald's.

tranquility (tran-KWIH-luh-tee) *n*. peacefulness; calmness

Turmoil turned to **tranquility** after the children went to sleep.

Keesha loves to end the day **tranquilly**, with a good book or some soothing music.

The water was so **tranquil** you could see your reflection in it.

uniformity (yoo-nuh-FOR-muh-tee) *n*. sameness; regularity

The boys were the picture of **uniformity**: all wore oversize pants, long T-shirts, baseball caps, and sneakers.

Carla became depressed over the **uniformity** of her days. She felt as though she were stuck in a rut.

Because every day was **uniformly** sunny, Gary yearned for some rain.

vilify (VIH-luh-fie) *vb*. to slander or defame someone's name or reputation

By calling him a "shiftless monster," the principal **vilified** the boy who had pulled the false alarm.

The newspapers **vilified** Patty, but the fact is that she had been falsely charged with the burglary.

Jay Leno and the other late night comedians **vilified** the president for a slip of the tongue.

whimsical (HWIM-zih-kul) *adj*. fanciful; changeable; mercurial

Dave's **whimsical** imagination enables him to tell the most amazing and entertaining stories.

The tale is based on the **whimsical** idea of a man who remains young while his portrait on the wall grows old.

Ms. Scotch declined to accept Nina's **whimsical** reason for being late. "Sorry," she said, "abduction by extraterrestrials is not an authorized excuse."

MEMORY TIPS

Use these mnemonics (memory devices) to boost your vocabulary. Make up your own memory clues for words in this lesson that are challenging for you. Add these tips—and your own—to your Vocabulary Notebook.

uniformity Think of the *uniform* worn by a student who attends a private high school. Students in *uniforms* create an outward appearance of sameness, or **uniformity**.

vilify Use this chant to remind you that **vilify** means *to slander or defame someone's name*. "**Vilify** the villain! **Vilify** the villain! **Vilify** the villain!" After all, if someone's name and reputation are to be marred (spoiled), why not the town villain?

MATCHING

Match the vocabulary words in Column A with *one or more* of their defining characteristics appearing in Column B.

Column A	Column B
1. recount	a. imaginative
2. vilify	b. hard work
3. querulous	c. calmness
4. scrutinize	d. grow strongly
5. saturate	e. soak completely
6. whimsical	f. to go beyond
7. tranquility	g. tell a story
8. uniformity	h. hesitant
9. thrive	i. to slander
10. rigor	j. sameness
11. surpass	k. examine closely
12. tentative	l. complaining

SENTENCE COMPLETION

Remember: Answer choices can be the lesson words themselves, or words that appear in definitions or Memory Tips. Select a word form and part of speech that fit correctly within the sentence.

1. Phillip appears to be _____ his reading assignment very carefully; he is highlighting the important parts, taking notes, and writing comments in the margin.
   (surpassing, scrutinizing, vilifying, thriving, recounting)

2. To more than survive, to _____ to their utmost potential, children require attention, love, praise, nutritious food, and fun exercise.
   (saturate, whimsy, thrive, uniformly, recount)

3. Melissa's colorful clothes, butterfly pins, and collection of fuzzy animal slippers reflect her _____ nature, which is indicative of her fanciful thinking.
   (tranquil, whimsical, tentative, querulous, rigorous)

4. In order to bestow her home with a sense of _____, Mrs. Pierra keeps her counters tidy, nurtures several green plants, and plays CDs with the sounds of running water.
   (severity, tentativeness, scrutiny, uniformity, tranquility)

5. Grandma Laura loved to _____ heartwarming stories of the good old days: her upbringing in Astoria, Queens; her running an active bar and grill; and living in close proximity to her sisters and extended family.
   (vilify, thrive, recount, scrutinize, surpass)

WORDS IN CONTEXT

Based on the context in which each **bold** word is used, identify the word usage of each sentence as either C (Correct) or I (Incorrect).

1. Expressing your fashion sense can be achieved through a school dress code of **uniformity**.

2. Every night Tanya would **scrutinize** her face for breakouts and blemishes. She'd stay in front of the mirror for close to an hour.

3. Dorothy, a woman who prides herself on her fine reputation, became sorrowful when she learned that the town gossip was **vilifying** her good name.

4. As a mother of five, Ms. Jallow's days are **saturated** with food shopping, doing laundry, and attending to the social calendar.

5. Hannah's **whimsical** daydreams included dreams of living in Paris and visions of being a famous fashion model.

aggregate audacious aviary complementary debunk discrepancy eclectic excerpt glacial

---

aggregate (A-grih-gut) *n.* a sum total or mixture

Concrete consists of an **aggregate** of sand, gravel, Portland cement, and water.

An **aggregate** of minority groups now makes up the majority of California's population.

An **aggregation** of disgruntled citizens mounted a rebellion against Mayor Meyer and threw the rascal out.

audacious (aw-DAY-shus) *adj.* very bold

More **audacious** than wise, Marvin daringly told the assistant principal to mind his own business.

In an **audacious** move, Jodi bucked the odds and scored the winning three-pointer at the buzzer.

Juan struck me as a meek and timid fellow. That he is **audacious** enough to wrestle with alligators is amazing.

aviary (AY-vee-er-ee) *n.* an enclosed space for birds

The new **aviary** at the zoo contains 200 different kinds of birds.

As Lucy walked through the **aviary**, a white dove landed on her shoulder.

This **aviary** contains birds of prey. The other one houses songbirds from all over the world.

complementary (kahm-pluh-MEN-tree) *adj*. serving to complete another

The couple's talents **complement** each other. She raises vegetables and he cooks them.

The art curriculum includes a course in abstract painting that is **complemented** by a course in realistic drawing and painting.

Our whirlwind visit to dorms and classrooms was **complemented** by a Q and A session in the college chapel.

debunk (dee-BUNGK) *vb*. to prove wrong or false

The photo of an alleged UFO was **debunked** by the man who threw a frisbee up in the air for the photographer.

Old wives tales are continuously **debunked** by modern research.

The claim that Mallory reached the summit of Mt. Everest was **debunked** by an analysis of the photos.

discrepancy (dis-KREH-pun-see) *n*. a difference or inconsistency

Julian was upset by the **discrepancy** between the amount of his actual paycheck and what he had been told he would earn.

A **discrepancy** in the suspect's story led the detectives to conclude that he was lying.

I never fail to find a **discrepancy** in my checkbook between my figures and the bank's figures.

eclectic (eh-KLEK-tik) *adj*. taken from many different sources

On my street the houses are **eclectic**. Each one is built in a different architectural style.

Mom prefers an **eclectic** assortment of furniture, regardless of its condition or style.

This dinner is **eclectic**: egg rolls, borscht, pizza, and crème brûlée for dessert.

excerpt (EK-surpt) *n*. a portion of a text or musical piece that is taken, or extracted, from the whole

The critical reading section of the verbal SAT contains short **excerpts** taken from books, periodicals, and speeches.

The medley consists of several **excerpts** from Broadway musical comedies.

In preparing the case, Shazia **excerpted** articles from the U.S. Constitution.

glacial (GLAY-shul) *adj*. very cold or very slow moving (in both cases, like a glacier)

Quentin built his house at a **glacial** pace; it took him 12 years.

The shopkeeper's **glacial** stare made me feel unwelcome, so I left.

Although I wore several layers of clothing, the **glacial** wind chilled me to the bone.

MEMORY TIPS

Use these mnemonics (memory devices) to boost your vocabulary. Make up your own memory clues for words in this lesson that are challenging for you. Add these tips—and your own—to your Vocabulary Notebook.

aggregate Do you remember what the root "gregis" means? Think back to *gregarious*, which appeared in Lesson 6. "Gregis" means *group* or *herd*. So, to **aggregate** is to collect and gather until a *group* is formed.

aviary If you are familiar with the word *aviation* (having to do with airplanes and flying), then you can link this knowledge to **aviary**, a place where birds fly around.

complementary Let the underlined portion of this word lead you to the word's meaning, *to complete*. Your math knowledge could help you here. Remember that **complementary** angles add up to 90 degrees. In a way, these angles *complete* each other in order to reach 90 degrees. Once again, the idea behind this memory tip is linking what you already know to something "new."

eclectic Let *eclectic* rhyme (slant rhyme, really) with "collected" or "selected." **Eclectic** items, after all, are *collected* or *selected* from various sources.

excerpt To remember the meaning of this word, it is helpful to know the prefix ex-. *Ex-* means "out," just like in ex̲it, ex̲punge, and ex̲ude. The Critical Reading sections of the SAT contain excerpts, pieces of writing taken *out* of the larger piece.

glacial Connect this word to glaci̲er, which is both cold and slow moving.

MATCHING

Match the vocabulary words or roots in Column A with *one or more* of their defining characteristics appearing in Column B.

Column A	Column B
1. discrepancy	a. freezing cold
2. audacious	b. enclosed space for birds
3. excerpt	c. a section from a piece of writing
4. aggregate	d. to prove false
5. gregis	e. difference
6. eclectic	f. selected from various good sources
7. complementary	g. a group or herd
8. aviary	h. bold
9. debunk	i. to gather
10. glacial	j. completing each other

SENTENCE COMPLETION

Remember: Answer choices can be the lesson words themselves, or words that appear in definitions or Memory Tips. Select a word form and part of speech that fit correctly within the sentence.

1. Janna moves around at such a (an) _____ pace that one can't help but wonder how she gets anything accomplished in a day.
   (avian, debunking, glacial, aggregate, eclectic)

2. With a flawless complexion that looks airbrushed, Gianna wears a pale peach lip gloss that _____ her peach blush beautifully, as if the two makeup items had been packaged to work together in exquisite, aesthetic harmony.
(complements, excerpts, debunks, aggregates, expunges)

3. With its recent acquisition of state grant funds, the garden center has just annexed a (an) _____ to its charming gazebo so that guests can watch the birds fly, preen, and sing their unique songs.
(debunk, excerpt, aggregate, discrepancy, aviary)

4. A savvy shopper, Noah detected a (an) _____ between the five items in his shopping bag and the *six* items listed on his cash register receipt.
(excerpt, discrepancy, debunk, audacity, complement)

5. Cynical about every theory and ideology she comes across, Mariella attempts to _____ the status quo every chance she gets.
(exude, aggregate, debunk, complement, excerpt)

WORDS IN CONTEXT

Based on the context in which each **bold** word is used, identify the word usage of each sentence as either C (Correct) or I (Incorrect).

1. The **aggregate** supply of apples picked by the children was more than their parents hoped for: 18 bushels!

2. Dr. Rain became irritated when the science experiment that was supposed to confirm his findings ended up **debunking** them.

3. Justin **excerpted** a quoted passage from the novel to demonstrate his theory.

4. Their opinions about weekend plans were **complementary**, and the two began quarreling into the wee hours of the morning.

5. Mr. Seymor's tie collection is **eclectic**. He purchases expensive ties in a variety of patterns and materials at upscale boutiques.

Lesson 35

EVEN MORE HOT WORDS

insuperable lithe misanthrope pitfall raze replete respite spurious vaporize

---

insuperable (in-SOO-pruh-bul) *adj.* unable to be overcome

Playing an **insuperable** team, we don't stand a chance in Saturday's game.

The odds seemed **insuperable**, but survivors were found in the rubble 10 days after the earthquake.

Napoleon's army was **insuperable** until it reached Moscow, where it first met defeat.

lithe (LITHE) *adj.* nimble and flexible; agile; supple

Do lots of stretching and stay away from fast food if you really want to be as **lithe** as a willow.

To be a ballerina, you must be lean and **lithe**.

Jason is a walking stiff on stage, but the role calls for an actor with a **lithe** body like Fred Astaire's.

misanthrope (MIH-sn-thrope) *n.* someone who dislikes all people

Hal has a **misanthropic** streak. He dislikes almost everyone.

Claire looks at everyone through rose-colored glasses. A dose of **misanthropy** might give her personality a bit more substance.

Rachel's statement that all men are vermin confirmed her status as a **misanthrope**.

pitfall (PIT-fawl) *n.* an unseen danger, risk, or drawback

The one **pitfall** in Doug's excellent plan is that it may cost too much.

The biggest **pitfall** Kerry found in going to college in Alaska was how much she missed her high school friends.

Beware of the **pitfalls** of sunbathing, especially the increased chance of developing skin cancer later in life.

raze (RAYZ) *vb.* to tear down; to destroy

The old Victorian house was **razed** to make room for a parking garage.

While **razing** the shed, Vickie made a big mistake. She tore down the walls before dismantling the roof.

During the slum-clearance project, more than 1,000 run-down buildings were **razed**.

replete (rih-PLEET) *adj.* filled-up; overflowing

Morticia cannot tell the truth. Her story is **replete** with outrageous exaggerations.

The new mall is **replete** with shops meant to attract fashion-conscious young women.

Although the film is **replete** with sex and violence, it got a "G" rating.

respite (RES-put) *n.* period of inactivity; a lull; a reprieve

Max's **respites** from work last longer than the work itself. At this rate, he'll never finish painting the room.

The rain took a **respite** at midday and permitted the children to go out and play.

If Holly doesn't take a periodic **respite** while driving long distances, she goes stir crazy.

spurious (SPYOOR-ee-us) *adj.* false; counterfeit; lacking logic; specious

In our earth science lab, we had to determine which fossils were genuine and which were **spurious**.

McCall said he was the author of the poem, but his claim was **spurious**. The actual author was McCarthy.

Lewis and Clark discovered that the rumors of an all-water route to the Pacific were **spurious**.

vaporize (VAY-puh-rize) *vb.* to turn to vapor, foam, or mist

> Zap! The space ranger **vaporized** the alien creature into a fine mist.

> Who doesn't know that water begins to **vaporize** when it starts to boil?

> As the dry ice **vaporized**, the actors on stage disappeared in clouds of smoke.

MEMORY TIPS

Use these mnemonics (memory devices) to boost your vocabulary. Make up your own memory clues for words in this lesson that are challenging for you. Add these tips—and your own—to your Vocabulary Notebook.

lithe Let li- lead you to limber. Recite this alliterative phrase three times: "long-legged limber ballerina!"

misanthrope The root at the center of this word holds part of its meaning. "Anthrop" means *man*. Add the prefix *mis-* (meaning "hatred" in this case), and the full meaning of **misanthrope** becomes clear: "hater of mankind." Additional words containing *anthrop* (man) include: anthropology and philanthropic (Lesson 8).

raze Let the irony of this word work for you. In other words, the meaning of **raze** is the *opposite* of what you'd expect. Since **raze** sounds like *raise*, you might think it has to do with building up or erecting a structure. Instead, **raze** means the opposite: to tear down to the ground.

respite How exciting! The meaning is actually *in the word*. In your Vocabulary Notebook, underline the parts of this word that spell *rest*.

MATCHING

Match the vocabulary words or roots in Column A with *one or more* of their defining characteristics appearing in Column B.

Column A	Column B
1. insuperable	a. filled to the brim
2. vaporize	b. to turn into some sort of mist
3. raze	c. a break in activity
4. pitfall	d. flexible
5. lithe	e. unbeatable
6. respite	f. fake
7. spurious	g. to tear down
8. misanthrope	h. man
9. anthrop	i. person who dislikes others
10. replete	j. a trap or danger

SENTENCE COMPLETION

Remember: Answer choices can be the lesson words themselves, or words that appear in definitions or Memory Tips. Select a word form and part of speech that fit correctly within the sentence.

1. _____ may lead to misery; after all, how happy can people be if they go around finding fault with everyone they meet?
   (Respite, Pitfall, Philanthropy, Razing, Misanthropy)

2. After two hours of yoga, Miranda decided to take a _____ and watch a morning talk show while sipping a chocolate protein shake.
   (raze, respite, lithe, pitfall, spurious)

3. _____ with all the material possessions she could ever hope for, Felicia looked away from her brimming clothes closet and jewelry drawer, and started to contemplate the spiritually fulfilling and gratifying aspects of life.
(Lithe, Specious, Razed, Replete, Vaporized)

4. Even though baked ziti seems a dieter's nightmare, the part-skim mozzarella and whole wheat penne pasta make it rather _____ to the waistline.
(misanthropy, innocuous, lithe, reprieve, nimble)

5. Some video games marked "Teen" and "Mature" are so dramatic and violent that one minute the player blows up a military fortress and the next minute he _____ an enemy soldier.
(repletes, vaporizes, reprieves, pitfalls, spurious)

WORDS IN CONTEXT

Based on the context in which each **bold** word is used, identify the word usage as either C (Correct) or I (Incorrect).

1. **Insuperable** Ivan is a giant who cannot be overcome.

2. The demolition crew followed their order to **raze** the shabby building.

3. All the participants praised the plan's major **pitfall**.

4. It is important for weight lifters to be **replete** so they can do deep squats while holding 50-pound weights.

5. The woman **vaporized** herself with the latest perfume.

Review Exercises / Lessons 31–35

VOCABULARY-IN-CONTEXT PARAGRAPH

The paragraph below primarily features words that appear in vocabulary lessons 31–35. For added reinforcement, additional vocabulary words from other lessons may appear in the paragraph. In those cases, the lesson number in which the words appear is indicated within parentheses. In light of the context, the words' meanings should be clear. If you are uncertain about particular meanings, however, take a moment to review the word's definition and illustrative sentences, as provided within the referenced lessons.

Lessons 31–35: Manhattan Studio

In decorating her new Manhattan studio, the college student *aspired* to create a space that was sleek, uncluttered, and contemporary. Still, she wanted her apartment to have a sense of warmth and not a *glacial* atmosphere. So she chose a cool, yet warm, color palette that included earth-tones of brown, brown-black, and assorted mineral blues. This blend of *complementary* tones proved to be the perfect *antidote* to a stressful day of back-to-back classes and exams, a place to take a *respite* from the hustle-bustle of the day and to *gratify* one's need for *tranquility*. *Replete* with an *eclectic* décor and some *whimsical* touches like a glass lamp base filled with shells, the studio pleased her *aesthetic* (Lesson 29). Placed in vases on tabletops, vibrant and exotic bird feathers broke up both the *homogeneity* and the *uniformity* of color.

SENTENCE COMPLETION

Note: On the new SAT (March 2016 and forward), multiple-choice sentence completion questions have been eliminated. However, sentence completion questions remain in this book as a vocabulary-strengthening exercise. Make flashcards for the words that are unknown or unfamiliar to you.

Read the sentence through carefully. Then from the five vocabulary words given in parentheses, circle the word that fits *best*.

1. Because of the prizefighter's awesome competitive record, his fans called him "The _____."
   (Aggregate, Eclectic, Lofty, Insuperable, Ponderous)

2. Exotic and tropical birds flew around the _____.
   (nurture, aviary, tentative, abridge, glacial)

3. Unfortunately, television programming is _____ with violence; there seems to be fighting, shooting, or bloodshed on the majority of channels.
   (surpassed, querulous, hampered, intrepid, saturated)

4. Big Ego Bruce _____ on flattery.
   (thrives, vilifies, scrutinizes, razes, pitfalls)

5. Despite Tina and Nick's _____, they did not speak a word to each other.
   (respite, proximity, candor, antidote, autonomy)

6. After five long days of sightseeing, the Hillers took a (an) _____ at the hotel pool, where they lounged all day long.
   (raze, linger, mock, respite, excerpt)

7. The aching pit in Ava's stomach served as a (an) _____ sign of something ill-fated to come.
   (opportunist, ominous, inception, aggregate, robust)

8. Chiropractor Rick believes that one of his professional missions is to _____ old wives' tales and replace these spurious theories with sound biological knowledge.
   (vilify, hamper, debunk, scrutinize, nurture)

9. Gretta's supple, _____ body helps her achieve each grace-
   ful pose on the balance bar and uneven bars.
   (lithe, whimsical, thriving, glacial, eclectic)

10. Lacking a green thumb, Jillian selects only the most _____
    ferns to keep as houseplants.
    (tentative, bolstered, autonomous, hardy, complementary)

11. Preferring peace to pandemonium, Lana _____ when moments
    of _____ grace her day.
    gratifies...discrepancy
    razes...whimsicality
    bolsters...candor
    thrives...tranquility
    nurtures...proximity

12. Miranda's interior decorating style is _____ and imaginative;
    in one corner of her living room, a bamboo _____ houses
    silk birds, while in the opposite corner a fake palm tree displays a
    bunch of painted coconuts!
    complementary...bolster
    whimsical...aviary
    lofty...antidote
    autonomous...abridge
    aggregate...homogeneity

MATCHING

How well do you recall what you learned in the Memory Tips sections of the past five lessons? Try this matching exercise to find out.

Column A	**Column B**
1. the prefix *ex-*, as in expunge or exculpate	a. a herd or group
2. a synonym for meticulous	b. relating to planes and flying
3. the prefix *auto-*, as in *auto*immune or *auto*mation	c. man
4. the Greek root *gregis*	d. out
5. aviation	e. fastidious
6. the root *anthrop*	f. self

Lesson 36

LITERARY TERMS THAT ARE HELPFUL TO KNOW

Vocabulary and the New SAT Essay

Given the SAT's new essay format, the vocabulary and rhetorical techniques of authors' craft that are covered in this lesson are more important than ever. Students will be provided with an essay prompt. This piece of writing will be preceded by directions similar to the following:

As you read the Source Text (provided passage) below, consider how the author uses

- evidence, such as examples or facts, to substantiate claims.
- reasoning to develop ideas and to relate evidence and claims.
- persuasive or stylistic features, such as diction (precise and effective word choice) or pathos (appeals to audience's emotions) to strengthen the power of the expressed ideas.

Write an essay in which you explain how the author formats and builds his or her argument to persuade readers that [author's claim will be inserted here]. In your essay, analyze how the author uses one or more of the features listed above (or features of your own choice) to strengthen the logic and persuasiveness of [his/her] argument. Be sure that your analysis of the provided passage focuses on the most relevant aspects of the passage. Your essay should not explain whether you agree with the author's claims, but rather explain how the author effectively builds an argument to persuade [his/her] audience.

The words in this lesson will help you as you write your essay. Sometimes they appear in the answer choices in the reading questions or within the reading passages themselves. These literary terms can sharpen your performance on the verbal sections of the SAT. Learn them for the test; learn them for life!

allusion anecdote catharsis euphemism hyperbole irony metaphor oxymoron parable parody pathos prose satire vignette

---

allusion (uh-LOO-zuhn) *n.* an indirect reference, often to a character or theme found in some work of literature

See Lesson 29, Tricky Twins and Triplets

anecdote (A-nik-dote) *n.* a short autobiographical account or snippet from someone's past, usually humorous

A born storyteller, June glibly recounts one **anecdote** after the next, ranging from her grammar school days to the shenanigans that took place during her first weeks as a bank employee.

I can tell a lighthearted **anecdote** about my most embarrassing moment, but you cannot tell one about the latest Congressional proceedings.

Do not confuse **anecdotes**—mini-autobiographical tales—with anti-dotes, which are measures that counteract poisons.

catharsis (kuh-THAR-sus) *n.* an emotional cleansing or release of emo-tional tensions, fears, or pity

The dramatic and stirring final scenes of *King Kong* led many view-ers, who were filled with a mixture of strong emotion, to experience **catharses**.

Paul reports that intense crying allows him a **catharsis** that leaves him feeling refreshed and renewed.

People who regularly watch tear-jerkers and tragedies benefit from the **cathartic** experience of purging pent-up, potentially toxic emo-tions.

euphemism (YOO-fuh-mih-zum) *n.* a more pleasant word or phrase that replaces another that is too direct, distasteful, or offensive.

The gentler-sounding phrase "passed away" is a **euphemism** for "died."

Speaking **euphemistically**, Auntie Mabel frequently remarked that her nephew was "vivacious," instead of "hyperactive."

Preferring **euphemistic** language, Leyla encouraged her young sons to say, "I need to use the restroom," instead of "I gotta go poop!"

hyperbole (high-PUR-buh-lee) *n.* an exaggeration used to create an effect

"It's so hot, my skin is melting," commented Dina, who habitually spoke in **hyperboles**.

Again expressing herself with **hyperbole**, Dina added, "In order to cool off, I think I'll have an ice cream cone stacked twenty scoops high!"

"Cut back on the sweets," her husband chimed in. "Yesterday you ate enough sugar to fill a house!" he said **hyperbolically**.

irony (EYE-ruh-nee) *n.* an unexpected outcome or unanticipated twist of events presented in literature and in life

In Cinderella, the sought-after prince ends up with the lowly maid-servant; how **ironic**!

The **ironic** twists and turns of the plot kept the readers glued to the unpredictable storyline.

What an **irony**: the class clown, who never spoke a serious sentence in his life, was elected President of the Student Council!

metaphor (MEH-tuh-for) *n.* a figurative device in which a direct comparison is made, without using *like* or *as*

"Ian, if you can describe your glass bottom boat ride in terms of a **metaphor**, then you will surely achieve an original description," his teacher commented. Ian tried, "The floor of the glass bottom boat is a magnifying glass skimming the sea."

Diana asked the teacher, "Can't a hot cantaloupe serve as a **metaphor** for the setting sun?"

Coming across as a romantic poet, Piero spoke to his girlfriend in **metaphors**: "Your eyes are flawless diamonds, and your hair is golden threads!"

oxymoron (ahk-see-MOR-ahn) *n.* contradictory terms, appearing side by side, used for rhetorical effect

Popular examples of **oxymorons** include "jumbo shrimp" and "deafening silence."

In Shakespeare's play about ill-fated lovers, Romeo speaks in **oxymorons** when he exclaims, "O loving hate! O heavy lightness!"

The dog owner was offended, even though the passerby used a seemingly ambiguous **oxymoron** when he said the goofy-looking dog was "pretty ugly."

parable (PA-ruh-bul) *n.* a brief story, told or written in order to teach a moral lesson

The Bible is filled with **parables**, which are intended to teach readers how to live and treat others.

Grandmother's stories of her youth were not only entertaining, but they were also instructive, for she spoke to her grandchildren in **parables**.

Some literary critics believe that the classic novella, *The Pearl*, by John Steinbeck, is a **parable** that teaches readers the values of what is worth having in life.

parody (PA-ruh-dee) *n.* a work that imitates the style of another literary work; may be mocking or amusing; short, humorous parodies can be called spoofs

Some literary critics contend that George Orwell's fiction work, *Animal Farm,* is actually a **parody** of the Bolshevik Revolution.

To **parody** e.e. cummings' poetry writing style, the ninth grader wrote a free verse poem with little regard for the conventions of spelling, punctuation, and sentence structure.

Some argue that *Spaceballs* **parodies** outer space action-dramas such as *Star Trek* and *Star Wars*.

pathos (PAY-thohs) *n.* the quality of a piece of writing that evokes pity, sympathy, or some other strong emotional response in the reader

According to Aristotle, there are three strategies that are used in persuasive rhetoric: ethos, logos, and **pathos**.

The author inundated his writing with such a heavy dose of **pathos** that the short story became less of a social drama and more of a tearjerker!

To stir their readers' emotions, prose writers might infuse a heaping spoonful of **pathos** into their stories.

prose (PROZE) *n.* writing that is not poetry or rhyming verse (i.e., a novel, play, or essay)

Dina dabbles in poetry, yet she is more of a **prose** writer, turning out one short story or novella after another.

Prose writers should master the literary elements of rising action, climax, and falling action, in order to shape poignant stories.

Iambic pentameter, rhyming couplets, and free verse are of little concern to the writers of **prose**.

satire (SA-tire) *n.* a literary work, often humorous, intended to ridicule the public figures, behaviors, or political situations presented or alluded to in the work

In order to write **satire**, one needs to have something to say and the savvy to say it with wit and humor.

Jonathan Swift's classic, *Gulliver's Travels,* is a widely-read **satire** that mocks the English, portraying them as small-minded when it comes to both thinking and action.

Given his subtle yet pointed sense of humor, Ivan would make a good **satirist**.

vignette (vin-YET) *n.* a brief descriptive passage in writing

With a detailed description of the green-and-white striped awning, the wrought iron bistro tables, and the baskets of freshly-baked rolls, the travel writer depicted a colorful **vignette** of the *trattoria,* an outdoor Italian eatery.

In just two highly-illustrative paragraphs, the cross-cultural writer portrayed a vivid **vignette** of a traditional Japanese tea ceremony.

In John Steinbeck's *The Pearl,* the author uses **vignettes** to dramatically depict the seafaring life of a Mexican pearl diver.

MEMORY TIPS

Use these mnemonics (memory devices) to boost your vocabulary. Make up your own memory clues for words in this lesson that you find tricky. Add these tips—and your own—to your Vocabulary Notebook. When coming up with memory aids, think outside the box!

euphemism The prefix *eu-* means "good, well." As you recall from this lesson, a **euphemism** is a good way (nice way) of saying something that might otherwise come across as harsh or unpleasant. Words that begin with *eu-* are positive value words; for example, eulogy, euphoria, and euphonious! In Homer's grand epic, *The Odyssey,* you might recall reading about Eumaois, the *good* swineherd!

hyperbole You've heard of hyperactive kids, right? **Hyper**active means *over* active. Well, the prefix *hyper* means "over and above." Link that to **hyperbole**, *overly* stated or exaggerated.

pathos The Greek *pathos* means suffering; in contemporary usage, it means pity or compassion. If you think of all the words you already know that contain the root of this word—em**path**y, sym**path**y, **path**etic—then *pathos* won't seem like a new word after all.

MATCHING—PART I

Match the vocabulary words in Column A with their definitions appearing in Column B.

Column A	Column B
1. parody	a. reference to a literary work
2. anecdote	b. nice way of saying something unpleasant
3. pathos	c. brief yet vivid description
4. euphemism	d. emotional appeal to readers
5. allusion	e. a brief account of an incident
6. vignette	f. work that pokes fun at another work
7. satire	g. work that ridicules a person, institution, or social practice

MATCHING—PART II

Match the vocabulary words in Column A with their definitions appearing in Column B.

Column A

8. irony

9. metaphor

10. oxymoron

11. catharsis

12. hyperbole

13. parable

14. prose

Column B

h. emotional cleansing

i. exaggeration

j. unexpected outcome or event

k. essays, novels, short stories

l. direct comparison

m. combination of opposites

n. story with a moral lesson

SENTENCE COMPLETION

Remember: *Answer choices can be the lesson words themselves, or words that appear in definitions or Memory Tips. Select a word form and part of speech that fit correctly within the sentence.*

1. Never trying his hand at haiku or rhyming verse, Tanner is a dedicated writer of _____ who prefers paragraphs, plot lines, and fully-developed characterization.
   (metaphor, vignette, catharsis, prose, euphemism)

2. When I was a child, my mother slipped a magazine headline into my Christmas stocking that read, "Happiness is a warm puppy." This _____, warm and joyful, stays with me, as I remember the elation I felt when we picked up my white miniature poodle, Taffy, just a few days later.
   (irony, metaphor, parable, parody, oxymoron)

3. Jack has a pile of work the size of Olympus Mons, an enormous mountain found on Mars that is three times higher than Mount Everest! This statement is an example of _____.
   (satire, euphemism, parody, allusion, hyperbole)

4. When Ernest wrote his adventure story, he included several _____ to the great heroes, monsters, and battles that appear in both Mesopotamian myth and the Epic Tales of Gilgamesh.
(oxymorons, allusions, ironies, anecdotes, vignettes)

5. From milking the restless cows to hiding fresh-baked blueberry muffins under his T-shirt, Uncle Lester shares the most amusing _____ about his adventuresome boyhood spent on the farm.
(euphemisms, parables, pathos, anecdotes, catharses)

WORDS IN CONTEXT

Based on the context in which each **bold** word is used, identify the word usage as either C (Correct) or I (Incorrect).

1. "Frigid cold" is a sound example of an **oxymoron**.

2. **Prose** writers regularly concern themselves with rhythm, rhyme scheme, and alliteration.

3. In order to bring about feelings of sympathy and compassion in readers, novelists infuse their stories with a moving dose of **pathos**.

4. "It's raining cats and dogs" and "So hungry I could eat a horse" are examples of cliché **hyperboles**.

5. A secondary purpose of **satire** is for the author to indirectly poke fun at himself and his writing ability.

Lesson 37

ACT VOCABULARY: PROSE FICTION AND HUMANITIES

This lesson features vocabulary found within the Prose Fiction and Humanities reading genres of the ACT Reading Test. Vocabulary enhancement allows you, as a test taker, greater ease and clarity when reading. In turn, you will be able to answer the multiple-choice questions with greater speed and accuracy on the ACT Reading Test. A broader, richer vocabulary will also help you to write a more effective essay on the ACT Writing Test.

The vocabulary words listed are in order of their appearance, as found within the reading passages of all five tests contained in The Real ACT Prep Guide, 3rd Edition. *Four words have been selected from each reading theme. This Prose Fiction and Humanities lesson contains eight words. The Social Science and Natural Science lesson also contains eight words. (For more practice, Barron's* Hot Words for the ACT *provides comprehensive ACT vocabulary review.)*

---

anthology attribute connote dissonance
improvisation meander provocative retrospect

---

anthology (an-THAHL-uh-jee) *n.* a collection of short stories and/or poems; sometimes a collection of works of art or music

The young man's photograph, "Lone Seagull," was published in a hardcover **anthology** of poems and pictures relating to Long Island.

Dr. Painter's short literary works and essays make up her award-winning Italian prose collection in an **anthology** titled *A Woman's Voice.*

Titled "Today's Vibe," the **anthology** is geared toward a teen audience and contains short stories about shopping at American Apparel, attending concerts, posting on Facebook, and Tweeting.

attribute (A-tri-byoot) *n.* a characteristic, property, or quality of something or someone

A true gentleman, Sy is remembered for his many positive **attributes** that include a soft-spoken demeanor, a jovial personality, and a ready smile.

Among the university's most appealing **attributes** are a lush and sprawling campus, several large quads, and a new state-of-the-art business building.

For many, Moe's Southwest Grill possesses many **attributes** of a delicious dining experience: warm tortillas, delectable guacamole, and zesty salsa!

connote (kuh-NOWT) *vb.* to suggest or imply something beyond a word's literal or dictionary meaning

Although many regard "consequences" as negative outcomes, in certain contexts this term can actually **connote** positive results.

The term "home" often **connotes** a sense of familiarity, comfort, and warmth.

dissonance (DIS-uh-nuhnts) *n.* disagreement, discord, or conflict; unpleasant sounds, cacophony

Nina is a peacemaker; she'd rather walk away then engage in **dissonance**.

For individuals who thrive amid harmony, **dissonance** can be both physically and emotionally debilitating.

Dissonance in a relationship can be mitigated by each person overlooking the other person's faults while accentuating his or her best qualities.

improvisation (im-prah-vi-ZAY-shun) *n.* the act of making, creating, delivering, performing in an offhand, unrehearsed manner; performing extemporaneously; improv (abridged form—casual or slang)

The tour guide was animated and entertaining. She used **improvisation** to add a dramatic element to an otherwise mundane campus tour.

With a little **improvisation**, a backyard fire pit can become more than a fire pit: it can serve as a welcoming hearth for friendly storytelling or as a convenient repository for pistachio and sunflower seed shells.

meander (mee-AN-dur) *vb.* to walk, following a winding or complex course; to casually or aimlessly stroll along or wander without a definite or pressing destination

With walking-tour maps in hand, we **meandered** up and down the lush and intricate pathways that led to the main campus quad.

Searching for the perfect weekend outfits, Kerri and Nicole **meandered** around the mall for hours.

After Ella and Libby **meandered** along the waterside walkway, they took 89 steps down to the boardwalk then climbed a staircase leading to Sunset Park.

provocative (pruh-VA-kuh-tiv) *adj.* intending to excite, arouse interest, stimulate; inciting

Not only do comedians and musicians visit the campus but **provocative** movies and documentaries are featured at the student union.

One must engage his or her analytical faculties before succumbing to the **provocative** suggestions of others.

With the intention of **provoking** an altercation with her fair-weather friend, Hailey began to press all of her emotional buttons.

The **provocative** breaking news on the evening news channel kept the family glued to the screen.

retrospect (REH-truh-spekt) *n.* reflecting on and reviewing past actions in light of new information or with a new perspective

In **retrospect**, she wished she had spent her junior year abroad in London.

The adage says, "Hindsight is 20/20"; in other words, **retrospectively**, we tend to see the past with sharp clarity of mind.

Retrospection made her realize that afternoons spent shopping in Soho and strolling South Street Seaport were among her best summer highlights.

MEMORY TIPS

Use these mnemonics (memory devices) to boost your vocabulary. Make up your own memory clues for words in this lesson that are personally challenging. Add these tips—and your own—to your Vocabulary Notebook.

dissonance The prefix *dis-* means apart, not, the opposite. Consider this prefix in words such as **dis**cord or **dis**agreement. **Dissonance** is the *antithesis* (opposite of) accord and harmony.

retrospect The root words *spic, spec,* and *spect* pertain to seeing and looking (cons*pic*uous, in*spect*, *spect*ator). The prefix *retro-* means backward, back, or in reverse, as used in **retro**active. Knowledge of these stem words will help you piece together and recall this word's meaning.

MATCHING

Match the vocabulary words in Column A with *one or more* of their defining characteristics appearing in Column B.

Column A	Column B
1. anthology	a. bringing about interest, sparking ideas
2. meander	b. a defining characteristic or quality
3. attribute	c. a collection of poems or short works
4. retrospect	d. reflecting on past events, actions
5. provocative	e. to follow a nonlinear course of twists and turns

SENTENCE COMPLETION

Remember: Answer choices can be the lesson words themselves, or words that appear in definitions or Memory Tips. Select a word form and part of speech that fit correctly within the sentence.

1. The candidate's speech was _____, bringing about an uproar of emotion and protest from the audience.
   (retrospective, provocative, dissonant, connoting, improvisational)

2. His photograph, which was taken at the beach, was placed along-side a narrative poem that was compiled in a (an) _____ of short literary works about the environment.
(attribute, retrospect, connotation, antithesis, anthology)

3. One must be aware of how his or her dishonest and calculating actions can breed _____ even among those with whom we should be most closely bonded.
(antithesis, attributes, dissonance, retroactively, connotation)

4. _____ acting skills are perfected through off-the-cuff and spontaneous performances, whether they are brief skits or three-act plays.
(Meandering, Inciting, Connotative, Improvisational, Cacophonous)

5. Annabella's most endearing _____ is her willingness to see only the good in people and to overlook their limitations.
(attribute, cacophony, retrospection, improv, anthology)

WORDS IN CONTEXT

Based on the context in which each **bold** word is used, identify the word usage of each sentence as either C (Correct) or I (Incorrect).

1. Hanna's **retrospective** perspective allowed her to envision her life 10 years from now.

2. **Meandering** along the quiet and serpentine walking trail, the couple held hands and marveled at the deep, lush woods.

3. After three weeks of intense practice, their **improvisational** rendition of "Phantom of the Opera" turned out to be a masterpiece.

4. For some, the word "beach" **connotes** peaceful feelings of ease and images of beauty; for others, the term means baking in the sun like a chicken cutlet.

5. The purpose of the festive, lighthearted gathering was to promote **dissonance** among the guests.

Lesson 38

ACT VOCABULARY: SOCIAL SCIENCE AND NATURAL SCIENCE

This lesson features vocabulary found within the Social Science and Natural Science reading genres of the ACT Reading Test. Vocabulary enhancement allows you, as a test taker, greater ease and clarity when reading. In turn, you will be able to answer the multiple-choice questions with greater speed and accuracy on the ACT Reading Test. A broader, richer vocabulary will also help you to write a more effective essay on the ACT Writing Test.

The vocabulary words listed are in order of their appearance, as found within the reading passages of all five tests contained in The Real ACT Prep Guide, 3rd Edition. *Four words have been selected from each reading theme. The Prose Fiction and Humanities lesson contains eight words. This Social Science and Natural Social Science lesson also contains eight words. (For more practice, Barron's* Hot Words for the ACT *provides comprehensive ACT vocabulary review.)*

> **anomalies bias paragon prototype**
> **sacrilegious speculate streamline subjective**

---

anomalies (uh-NAH-muh-lees) *n.* rarities; things or people that deviate from the normal; deviations

His reticent personality and slow-moving manner made him an **anomaly** among his garrulous, fast-moving family members.

Despite the advanced technological age, genetic and anatomical **anomalies** continue to astound even the most experienced and well-trained biologists and doctors of today.

Both Tino and Baci are **anomalies** in the world of dogs that enjoy spending time running and lounging outdoors. Neither pet stays outside longer than it takes to do his business before he comes running back to the kitchen door.

bias (BIE-us) *n.* an opinion or one-sided outlook

Both the Writing multiple-choice questions on the SAT and the English multiple-choice questions on the ACT exhibit a clear **bias** toward language economy.

Lucky for him, his lifestyle **bias** is slanted toward activity rather than the sedentary existence of a couch potato.

To avoid **bias** among the voters, they should represent a cross-section of the community members.

paragon (PA-ruh-gahn) *n.* someone or something that is the very best model or example; a prime example; archetype

Lucy is a **paragon** of politeness, while Bruce is an archetype of curtness.

An esteemed **paragon** of fairness and goodwill, the high school teacher offers extra help every day after school, allows rewrites on term papers, and drops each student's lowest quiz grade.

Striving to be **paragons** was counterproductive for the women. As their true and fallible selves were unknown to others, authentic friendships could not be formed.

prototype (PRO-tuh-tipe) *n.* the original form of something that has essentially the same features and characteristics of later forms of that same type; the epitome

The original test-day kit **prototype** contained a Vitamin E lip balm, a vitamin C lollipop, and a roll of Mentos mints.

Before acquiring a patent, the inventor must create a tangible **prototype** of his or her innovation.

Using stretchable, patterned fabrics, Dana created several **prototypes** of stylish book covers that serve as fashion accessories as well as literacy aids.

sacrilegious (sa-cruh-LIH-jus) *adj.* disrespectfully treating something that individuals regard as sacred or holy; blasphemous

It is **sacrilegious** for an individual to be ungenerous with his or her help and time while, at the same time, claiming to be spiritually magnanimous.

Sacrilegious acts are revealed in the end, exposing their lack of truth and integrity.

For the ice-cream lover, denaturing those holy scoops with sprinkles, melted marshmallow, and gummy candies is a culinary **sacrilege**.

speculate (SPE-kyuh-layt) *vb.* to wonder, to guess, to put forth an opinion; to conjecture

Given her son's proclivity for science and interest in health, the mother **speculated** that her son would make a fine radiologist or anesthesiologist.

Given that Panera Bread is one of their daughter's favorite places for lunch, the parents **speculated** that there was a good chance they'd bump into Jodi and her friends when the parents stopped at Panera for a quick bite to eat.

streamline (STREEM-line) *vb.* to simplify a procedure or process to make more effective

Storing away surplus supplies, the pair **streamlined** the office so that it was an aesthetically pleasant and functional work space.

To **streamline** their business's scheduling requirements, the owners devised a three-step process to confirm and document client appointments.

A simple Excel spreadsheet **streamlined** their business activity, keeping all pertinent information and transactions in one place.

subjective (sub-JEK-tiv) *adj.* based on opinions, personal bias

What makes a college appealing is truly **subjective**. One high school senior might be drawn to a scenic, country campus; the other, a frenetic urban center.

Additional components of a great college experience are also **subjective**. For some it's the availability of internships; for others, the party scene.

Subjective assessments are based on opinions and subtleties rather than the numbers and data of objective analyses.

MEMORY TIPS

Use these mnemonics (memory devices) to boost your vocabulary. Make up your own memory clues for words in this lesson that are personally challenging. Add these tips—and your own—to your Vocabulary Notebook.

prototype Type is not a root word. Still, a *type* is a model or specimen having the qualities of some larger category. Link this basic understanding of type to **prototype**, which is similar, as an original model, standard example, or first full form of an original *type.*

speculate *Spec* as a root word means "to look" or "see." When a person speculates about something, someone, or some situation, he or she tries to see or imagine the situation in different ways and from different perspectives. Use *spec* as a link to the meaning of this word. *Spec* also appears in in**spec**t and **spec**tator.

MATCHING

Match the vocabulary words in Column A with *one or more* of their defining characteristics appearing in Column B.

Column A	Column B
1. sacrilege	a. a rarity; an aberrant or unusual factor
2. paragon	b. a personal leaning or opinion
3. streamline	c. to simplify a process
4. anomaly	d. irreverence toward that which is sacred or someone who is considered holy
5. bias	e. a model of perfection; supreme example

SENTENCE COMPLETION

Remember: Answer choices can be the lesson words themselves, or words that appear in definitions or Memory Tips. Select a word form and part of speech that fit correctly within the sentence.

1. In a family of pure and healthy eaters, fast-food-eating Tim was the
   _____.
   (sacrilege, bias, speculation, epitome, anomaly)

2. A _____ of tidiness and orderliness, Kayla had every piece of paper, mail, and clothing neatly placed in its appropriate spot in her impeccably organized house.
   (deviation, conjecturer, rarity, paragon, biased)

3. To _____ is to wonder about something or to put forth an opinion or guess.
   (epitome, bias, deviate, blasphemy, speculate)

4. Regardless of kind words, prayer, and visits to her house of worship, manipulative and irreverent actions make her a woman of undeniable _____.
   (streamlining, sacrilege, paragon, archetype, rarities)

5. _____ heroes such as Hercules and Braveheart are those who exhibit unsurpassed courage, experience great adversity, and reach beyond themselves to help and edify others.
   (Blasphemous, Prototype, Anomalous, Archetypal, Speculative)

WORDS IN CONTEXT

Based on the context in which each **bold** word is used, identify the word usage of each sentence as either C (Correct) or I (Incorrect).

1. Despite a plethora of studies and experiments, scientists continue to **speculate** about how the planets and solar system were formed.

2. A winter sports buff, the inventor's **prototype** represented his vision of the most smooth-moving and aerodynamically designed skis.

3. Basing his assertions on data, charts, and objective findings alone, Dr. Justin intermingles **subjectivity** and empirics in his neurological research.

4. Leah cannot speak of her godchild without **bias**; to Leah, her goddaughter is a perfect angel.

5. An **anomaly** among all the ordinary dogs in the family, the eight-year-old chocolate Labradoodle can dexterously and effortlessly open lever handle doors and turn on tub faucets!

Answer Key

LESSON 1

Matching

1. a   2. b   3. c   4. e   5. d

Sentence Completion

1. pithiness
2. Reticent
3. tersely
4. brevity
5. taciturn

Words in Context

1. C   2. I   3. C   4. C   5. I

LESSON 2

Matching

1. e   2. d   3. c   4. a   5. b

Sentence Completion

1. Prattling
2. loquacious
3. diffuse
4. Eloquence
5. digress

Words in Context

1. I   2. I   3. C   4. C   5. I

LESSON 3

Matching

1. a, b, d   2. b   3. a   4. e   5. c

Sentence Completion

1. disdainful
2. insolent
3. supercilious
4. swagger
5. Pretentious

Words in Context

1. I   2. I   3. C   4. C   5. I

LESSON 4

Matching

1. c, b   2. d, f   3. a, e   4. b   5. d, c   6. a, e

Sentence Completion

1. insipid
2. derivative
3. lackluster
4. clichés
5. Banal

Words in Context

1. I   2. I   3. I   4. C   5. I

LESSON 5

Matching

1. e   2. b   3. a   4. d   5. b

Sentence Completion

1. mediator
2. alleviates
3. conciliate
4. mitigate
5. mollify

Words in Context

1. I   2. C   3. C   4. I   5. C

REVIEW EXERCISES—LESSONS 1–5

Name That Cluster

1. V   2. III   3. II   4. I   5. IV

Sentence Completion

1. reticence
2. presumptuous
3. egoist
4. vapid
5. concise
6. mitigate . . . alleviated
7. laconic . . . voluble
8. quiescent
9. terse
10. concise

One Doesn't Belong

1. Garrulous means *talkative*.
2. Swagger means *to walk in a showy way*.
3. Taciturn means *silent*.
4. Allay means *to alleviate fear*.
5. Palliate means *to alleviate, soothe*.

LESSON 6

Matching

1. a   2. d   3. b   4. c   5. e

Sentence Completion

1. jocular
2. Cordial
3. convivial
4. levity
5. amiable

Words in Context

1. I   2. C   3. C   4. I   5. I

LESSON 7

Matching

1. b, d   2. e   3. c   4. b   5. a

Sentence Completion

1. contentious
2. predatory
3. belligerence
4. antagonist
5. disputatious

Words in Context

1. I 2. C 3. C 4. C 5. I

LESSON 8

Matching

1. a 2. e 3. b 4. c 5. c, d

Sentence Completion

1. Benevolent
2. Munificent
3. largess
4. altruism
5. magnanimity

Words in Context

1. I 2. I 3. C 4. C 5. C

LESSON 9

Matching

1. e, b 2. d 3. c 4. b 5. a

Sentence Completion

1. miserly
2. penurious
3. Avarice
4. austere
5. thrift

Words in Context

1. I 2. I 3. C 4. C 5. C

LESSON 10

Matching

1. d   2. a   3. c   4. b   5. e

Sentence Completion

1. conflagration
2. enigma
3. turbulence
4. labyrinth
5. confounding

Words in Context

1. I   2. I   3. C   4. C   5. C

REVIEW EXERCISES—LESSONS 6–10

Name That Cluster

1. III   2. II   3. V   4. IV   5. I

Sentence Completion

1. austerity
2. gregarious
3. contentious
4. precarious
5. levity
6. jocular . . . cantankerous
7. conflagration . . . adversity
8. cordial
9. jocular . . . levity
10. disputatious . . . belligerent

One Doesn't Belong

1. Altruistic means *kind, generous toward humankind.*
2. A conundrum is a *riddle.*
3. Squander means *to waste time or money.*
4. Mercenary means *seeking self-gain.*
5. A conflagration is an *inferno.*

LESSON 11

Matching

1. e   2. c   3. d   4. a   5. b

Sentence Completion

1. baneful
2. odious . . . nefarious
3. pernicious
4. virulent
5. detrimental

Words in Context

1. C   2. I   3. C   4. C   5. I

LESSON 12

Matching

1. c   2. b   3. d   4. a   5. e

Sentence Completion

1. upbraid
2. deride . . . castigate
3. reproval
4. rebuffed
5. chastised

Words in Context

1. I   2. I   3. C   4. C   5. I

LESSON 13

Matching

1. b   2. a, c, e   3. a   4. a, b, e   5. d

Sentence Completion

1. listless
2. indifferent
3. nonchalant . . . stolid
4. phlegmatic
5. apathetic

Words in Context

1. I   2. C   3. I   4. C   5. C

LESSON 14

Matching

1. c   2. d   3. a   4. b   5. e

Sentence Completion

1. stagnant
2. torpid . . . indolence
3. sedentary
4. languor
5. soporific

Words in Context

1. C   2. I   3. I   4. C   5. C

LESSON 15

Matching

1. d   2. b   3. e   4. c   5. a

Sentence Completion

1. toady
2. compliant . . . subservient
3. submissiveness
4. fawning
5. subordinate

Words in Context

1. I   2. I   3. I   4. C   5. C

REVIEW EXERCISES—LESSONS 11–15

Name That Cluster

1. II   2. I   3. V   4. III   5. IV

Sentence Completion

1. sedentary
2. sluggish
3. submissive
4. fawning
5. nefarious
6. lethargic . . . sedentary
7. apathetic . . . avid
8. compliant
9. deleterious
10. listlessness . . . lethargy

One Doesn't Belong

1. Iniquitous means *wicked*.
2. Subordinate means *acting inferior to another*.
3. Impassive means *without emotion*.
4. Obsequious means *acting in a slavish fashion*.
5. Berate means *to scold harshly*.

LESSON 16

Matching

1. c, e   2. a, b, d   3. a   4. c, e   5. b, d

Sentence Completion

1. fervent
2. ebullient
3. fanatical
4. Zealous
5. vibrant

Words in Context

1. I   2. I   3. I   4. C   5. C

LESSON 17

Sentence Completion

1. obstinate
2. Unyielding
3. recalcitrant
4. intractable
5. obdurate

Words in Context

1. C   2. I   3. I   4. I   5. C

LESSON 18

Matching

1. e   2. d   3. b   4. a   5. c   6. f

Sentence Completion

1. acoustical
2. din
3. mellifluous
4. shrill
5. discordant

Words in Context

1. C   2. C   3. C   4. I   5. C

LESSON 19

Matching

1. b   2. e   3. d   4. f   5. c   6. a

Sentence Completion

1. revere
2. panegyrized
3. venerable
4. adulation
5. accolades

Words in Context

1. C   2. C   3. I   4. C   5. C

LESSON 20

Matching

1. c   2. b, e   3. a   4. d   5. d

Sentence Completion

1. lavish
2. copious
3. prolific
4. myriad
5. ample

Words in Context

1. I   2. C   3. C   4. I   5. C

REVIEW EXERCISES—LESSONS 16–20

Name That Cluster

1. IV   2. II   3. V   4. I   5. III

Sentence Completion

1. venerated
2. ebullient
3. mellifluous
4. din
5. avid
6. discordant . . . mellifluous
7. lavish . . . obstinate
8. exuberant
9. myriad
10. surfeit . . . profuse

One Doesn't Belong

1. Vociferous means *loud in terms of talking noisily.*
2. Effervescent means *bubbly and lively.*
3. Defiant means *disobedient.*
4. Recalcitrant means *defiant, stubborn.*
5. Surfeit means an *oversupply or surplus.*

LESSON 21

Matching

1. c   2. e   3. f   4. a   5. d   6. b

Sentence Completion

1. ravenous
2. Gluttonous
3. savory
4. culinary
5. abstemious

Words in Context

1. I   2. I   3. C   4. C   5. C

LESSON 22

Matching

1. d   2. h   3. g, a   4. c
5. e   6. f   7. b   8. h

Sentence Completion

1. meticulous
2. gingerly
3. scrupulous
4. Chary
5. vigilant

Words in Context

1. C   2. I   3. I   4. C   5. C

LESSON 23

Matching

1. e   2. e   3. c   4. a   5. b, d

Sentence Completion

1. nomadic
2. transitory
3. ephemeral
4. volatile
5. itinerant

Words in Context

1. C   2. C   3. C   4. I   5. C

LESSON 24

Matching

1. e   2. f   3. g   4. c   5. a   6. d   7. b

Sentence Completion

1. contemporary
2. relics
3. antediluvian
4. obsolete
5. unprecedented

Words in Context

1. C   2. C   3. I   4. C   5. I

LESSON 25

Sentence Completion

1. covert
2. surreptitiously
3. slyly
4. inconspicuous
5. stealthy . . . covert

Words in Context

1. I   2. C   3. C   4. I   5. I

REVIEW EXERCISES—LESSONS 21–25

Name That Cluster

1. IV   2. II   3. III   4. V   5. I

Sentence Completion

1. transient
2. culinary
3. gluttonous
4. conscientious
5. palatable
6. surreptitious . . . covert
7. spectacle . . . inconspicuous
8. heedful . . . delectable
9. Vigilant . . . emaciated
10. Gluttonous . . . voraciously

One Doesn't Belong

1. Savory means *tasty*.
2. Furtive means *sneaky, sly.*
3. Antediluvian means *very, very old.*
4. Evanescent means *short-lived.*
5. Obsolete means *outdated, no longer in use.*

LESSON 26

Matching

1. e   2. b   3. d   4. a   5. c   6. f

Sentence Completion

1. adversary
2. orators
3. raconteur
4. skeptic
5. charlatan

Words in Context

1. I   2. I   3. C   4. C   5. C

LESSON 27

Matching

1. c   2. a, d   3. b, a   4. a, d   5. e

Sentence Completion

1. trifling
2. petty
3. superficial
4. Incidental
5. trivial

Words in Context

1. C   2. C   3. I   4. C   5. C

LESSON 28

Matching

1. c, d   2. a   3. d   4. b   5. e

Sentence Completion

1. Acute
2. shrewd
3. prudence
4. ingenious
5. erudite

Words in Context

1. C   2. I   3. C   4. I   5. C

LESSON 29

Matching

1. d   2. e   3. c   4. a   5. b

Sentence Completion

1. Divergent
2. arid
3. allusions
4. convalesce
5. ambiguous

Words in Context

1. I   2. I   3. C   4. C   5. C

LESSON 30

Matching

1. f   2. c   3. a   4. b   5. e   6. d   7. g

Sentence Completion

1. intimating
2. indigent
3. obtuse . . . imprudent
4. indigenous
5. ponderous

Words in Context

1. C   2. C   3. I   4. I   5. C

REVIEW EXERCISES—LESSONS 26–30

Name That Cluster

1. IV   2. I   3. III   4. II

Sentence Completion

1. indigenous
2. artisan
3. intimidate
4. skeptic
5. Frivolous
6. virtuoso . . . charlatan
7. incisive . . . petty
8. ambiguous . . . obscure
9. indignant . . . ponderous
10. skeptic . . . ponderable
11. prudent . . . convalescence
12. artisan

One Doesn't Belong

1. Sagacious means *wise*.
2. Peripheral means *unimportant*, or *not central to the main point.*
3. Pariah means *a social outcast.*

LESSON 31

Matching

1. g   2. f   3. c   4. a   5. d
6. b   7. j   8. i   9. h   10. e

Sentence Completion

1. autonomous
2. antidote
3. bolster
4. abridge . . . gratify
5. candor

Words in Context

1. I   2. C   3. C   4. C   5. I

LESSON 32

Matching

1. k   2. b   3. g   4. i   5. c   6. e

7. a   8. h   9. d   10. j   11. f

Sentence Completion

1. mock
2. proximity
3. opportunist . . . hampering
4. hardy . . . intrepidly
5. linger

Words in Context

1. I   2. C   3. C   4. I   5. C

LESSON 33

Matching

1. g   2. i   3. l   4. k   5. e   6. a

7. c   8. j   9. d   10. b   11. f   12. h

Sentence Completion

1. scrutinizing
2. thrive
3. whimsical
4. tranquility
5. recount

Words in Context

1. I   2. C   3. C   4. C   5. C

LESSON 34

Matching

1. e   2. h   3. c   4. i   5. g

6. f   7. j   8. b   9. d   10. a

Sentence Completion

1. glacial
2. complements
3. aviary
4. discrepancy
5. debunk

Words in Context

1. C   2. C   3. C   4. I   5. C

LESSON 35

Matching

1. e   2. b   3. g   4. j   5. d

6. c   7. f   8. i   9. h   10. a

Sentence Completion

1. Misanthropy
2. respite
3. Replete
4. innocuous
5. vaporizes

Words in Context

1. C   2. C   3. I   4. I   5. I

REVIEW EXERCISES—LESSONS 31–35

Sentence Completion

1. Insuperable
2. aviary
3. saturated
4. thrives
5. proximity
6. respite
7. ominous
8. debunk
9. lithe
10. hardy
11. thrives . . . tranquility
12. whimsical . . . aviary

Matching

1. d   2. e   3. f   4. a

5. b   6. c

LESSON 36

Matching—Part I

1. f   2. e   3. d   4. b   5. a

6. c   7. g

Matching—Part II

8. j   9. l   10. m   11. h   12. i

13. n   14. k

Sentence Completion

1. prose
2. metaphor
3. hyperbole
4. allusions
5. anecdotes

Words in Context

1. I
2. I
3. C
4. C (hack means *unoriginal, played-out*)
5. I

LESSON 37

Matching

1. c   2. e   3. b   4. d   5. a

Sentence Completion

1. provocative
2. anthology
3. dissonance
4. Improvisational
5. attribute

Words in Context

1. I   2. C   3. I   4. C   5. I

LESSON 38

Matching

1. d   2. e   3. c   4. a   5. b

Sentence Completion

1. anomaly
2. paragon
3. speculate
4. sacrilege
5. Archetypal

Words in Context

1. C   2. C   3. I   4. C   5. C

Appendix A
Mini Vocabulary Clusters

Vocabulary is important not only for SAT preparation but also for lifelong writing and speaking skills. The bold titles, as shown below, could suffice as basic definitions. However, to get a sense of each word's particular usage, you should consult a dictionary or *Webster.com*. Each word also has its subtleties and nuances of meaning, which you can best understand through reading and hearing the word used correctly.

As you enrich your vocabulary, you will become a more eloquent speaker and a more competent writer. This revised edition of *HOT WORDS for the SAT* presents a plethora of bonus words to you.

Wise Sayings
adages
aphorism
axiom
maxim
proverb

High Point
acme
apex
apogee
peak
pinnacle
summit
zenith

Low Point
abyss
chasm
gorge
nadir

Prevent or Frustrate a Plan
baffle*
deter
foil
hamper
hinder
impede
obstruct
preclude
stymie
thwart

Confuse
baffle*
befuddle
bemuse
bewilder
confound
perplex

*Note the two distinct meanings of *baffle*.

Erase, Void, Get Rid Of
abolish
abrogate
annihilate
annul
efface
eradicate
expunge
nullify
obliterate
vanquish
void

Beginner
amateur
apprentice
fledgling
neophyte
novice
rookie
tyro

Small Amount or Quantity
dearth
deplete
devoid
paucity
scarcity
sparse

Lie, Avoid, or Stretch the Truth
embellish
embroider
equivocate
fabricate
prevaricate

Rest Period or Break
cessation
hiatus
lull
moratorium
reprieve
respite
siesta

Flexible
agile
elastic
limber
lithe
nimble
pliant
supple

Changeable
capricious
dynamic
erratic
fickle
mercurial
vacillating
volatile
whimsical

Appendix B
More Tricky Twins

My experience as a verbal tutor reveals to me—time and again—how even the most conscientious students can easily confuse words. Even honors students regularly confuse words that sound alike or words that look similar. That is why this edition of *Hot Words for the SAT* includes even more tricky twins (beyond Lessons 29 and 30). Challenge yourself to learn the different meanings and to master the spelling of these tricky twins.

Remember how effective flash cards, sticky notes, and daily review can be.

adept—skilled; competent
inept—unskilled; incompetent

amity—friendship; trust
enmity—hatred; bitter feeling

approbation—approval
opprobrium—shameful disgrace

avert—turn away
divert—amuse; entertain

bemoan—lament
bemuse—confuse; befuddle

capacious—spacious; having large capacity
rapacious—greedy; grasping

enervate—weaken
venerate—respect

effervescent—bubbly
evanescent—short-lived

flounder—flail uselessly or helplessly about, as if in quicksand
founder—fail; sink

hail—cheer for; acclaim
hale—healthy

impassive—apathetic; indifferent
impassioned—ardent; fervent

ingenious—creative
ingenuous—honest

innate—inborn
inane—senseless, silly
insane—having a mental disorder

invective—a vicious, verbal attack; tirade
inventive—creative; resourceful

lucid—clear; transparent
lurid—gruesome; violent

onus—a burden or responsibility
opus—a great work of music

paramount—of greater value
tantamount—of equal value

perquisite—a fringe benefit; frill
prerequisite—something required beforehand

picaresque—relating to adventure stories about rogues
picturesque—scenic

prodigal—wasteful
prodigious—very large

provincial—narrow-minded
providential—saving for future

seditious—rebellious
sedulous—hard-working; diligent

solicitude—concern
solitude—aloneness

temerity—reckless boldness
timidity—shyness

tonic—an invigorating drink
toxic—poisonous

voluble—talkative
voluminous—very large

Word Index